The Basic School

A COMMUNITY FOR LEARNING

ERNEST L. BOYER

THE CARNEGIE FOUNDATION
FOR THE ADVANCEMENT OF TEACHING
5 IVY LANE, PRINCETON, NEW JERSEY 08540

LIBRARY OF CONGRESS CATALOGING-IN-PUBLICATION DATA

Boyer, Ernest L.
    The basic school : a community for learning / Ernest L. Boyer.
        p. cm.
    Includes bibliographical references and index.
    ISBN 0-931050-48-0
    1. Education, Elementary—United States. 2. Educational change—
United States. I. Title
LA219.B69 1995
372.973-dc20   95-11506
                                              CIP

Second printing, 1995
Copies are available from

CALIFORNIA PRINCETON FULFILLMENT SERVICES
1445 Lower Ferry Road
Ewing, New Jersey 08618

TOLL-FREE: U.S. & Canada (800) 777-4726 FAX (800) 999-1958

PHONE (609) 883-1759 FAX (609) 883-7413

THE BASIC SCHOOL

CONTENTS

ACKNOWLEDGMENTS

I am deeply grateful as I reflect on the incalculable contributions of the colleagues and friends without whose time and effort this project could not have been completed. So many individuals have contributed to the work that led to *The Basic School* that I'm including a special section in the appendix to recognize each by name. But I wish to acknowledge here those whose efforts have been especially important.

I am most indebted to The Carnegie Foundation's Board of Trustees. I thank them for their unstinting commitment to the effort and for the consistent encouragement I've received. I take responsibility for the observations and conclusions presented here, but members of the Board must be acknowledged for their recognition of the importance of early education.

I also gratefully acknowledge the John D. and Catherine T. MacArthur Foundation for generous financial support. In particular, we thank John Corbally, former president, and Adele Simmons, current president. And Peter Gerber, director of the education program, was constantly encouraging and supportive and has my great gratitude.

From the earlier stages of the project, three colleagues receive my special gratitude. Dale Coye, Mary Huber, and Gene I. Maeroff helped lay the groundwork for this report through exhaustive research and writing. A study of the first years of formal learning was a new frontier for the Foundation, and these colleagues tirelessly explored the territory, writing extensively and well on every key aspect of elementary education. And more recently, Lee Mitgang also joined the effort, making very helpful contributions.

I owe a special debt to Vito Perrone, who contributed consequentially to *The Basic School* from the very first. Vito organized school visits, wrote initial drafts, critiqued ideas, always providing wise, insightful counsel. I am most grateful for his friendship and support.

I also express deep gratitude to my friend and colleague Robert Hochstein. Bob serves, always, as a key advisor, and his energy, skill, and commitment, both in shaping and in publicizing the work of the Foundation, cannot be overstated.

For her tireless work and dedication, I wish to thank Sally Reed, whose research and editing were absolutely crucial. She talked with people, visited schools, gathered data, critiqued material, and provided examples of best, current practice. She is also responsible for the extensive supporting documentation in the Notes section. Sally worked unceasingly to help keep this report moving forward, and I am deeply appreciative of the role she played.

Jan Hempel has been an important colleague, too. Once again she worked sensitively with the manuscript, making thoughtful editorial suggestions, and working diligently to prepare the report for publication, putting all of the separate pieces creatively together.

As *The Basic School* neared completion, we took the unusual step of creating a network of schools to begin to implement the priorities we were outlining. I am deeply grateful to The Ewing Marion Kauffman Foundation, in Kansas City, Missouri, for the generous grant that made it possible for us to move from thought to action. I am especially indebted to Robert B. Rogers, chairman and CEO, Susan Wally, and Mark Kenney, colleagues at the Kauffman Foundation.

My special thanks go as well to Mary Ellen Bafumo for directing the field project. Mary Ellen had already worked on various aspects of the Basic School project, and for the past year she has worked tirelessly and with meticulous professionalism to ensure the success of the first Basic Schools.

And on the other side of the partnership, I must single out for special recognition Alicia Thomas, principal of the Jackson-Keller Elementary School in San Antonio, Texas. Alicia's intelligent, energetic, and creative leadership moved her school in an extraordinary new direction, and this study has been improved immeasurably by the "laboratory" role the school has played in implementing the priorities of the Basic School. I'm especially grateful to the teachers at Jackson-Keller, who committed themselves to the vision of the Basic School three years ago and worked hard to bring this vision to life.

I also thank the staff and parents, too, for the support they've given the school. I further recognize the support from Richard Middleton, superintendent of The Northeast Independent School District in San Antonio. I express special gratitude to John Moore, chairman of the Department of Education at Trinity University, and Shari Albright, a professor at Trinity, for their outstanding work in developing a vital connection between the university and Jackson-Keller. And I appreciate, also, the teachers, administrators, and parents involved at all the other pilot schools.

I feel a very special sense of gratitude to my colleague and close friend Samuel G. Sava for the enormously valuable contribution he made to the creation of the Basic School. Because of his leadership and commitment, along with the help of Deborah Reeve and Gail Gross, the National Association of Elementary School Principals has been a partner in this project, a relationship that has meant more to me than I can say.

I wish to express deep thanks, too, to Richard Ferguson, president of ACT, for his valuable guidance, and for the great expertise we received from Cyndie Schmeiser, vice president, along with their team: Mary Schmidt, Mark Rekase, Suzanne Bottelli, Irene Connelly, Cindy Erenberger, Caryl Lyons, and Stan Ziewacz.

I recognize with gratitude, as well, the valuable contribution of the Council of Chief State School Officers, and in particular, the support of the project we have received from Gordon M. Ambach, executive director. This support has been particularly crucial in making the connections required by the network of pilot schools in the different regions of the country.

I must express my deepest gratitude to the Foundation staff for their dedication to this and to every project we undertake. Jeanine Natriello has my great appreciation for her extensive administrative work in support of the Basic School Network, as well as for her splendid management of the endless details around the release of this report and for her truly remarkable achievement in the final stages of the project, the production of the Basic School video and audio tapes.

Particularly for her work on the curriculum, I thank Carolyn Lieberg. Jack Osander and M. Kathryn Federici also contributed to our early work on the curriculum. Carol Tate and Johanna Wilson recently worked in depth on Basic School curriculum development.

Mary Jean Whitelaw skillfully directed the survey and data management work for the later stages of *The Basic School*, most recently the 1994 International Schooling Project, which is a survey of parents, teachers, and fifth-grade students in twelve countries around the world. Assisting Mary Jean are Lois Harwood and Craig Wacker. These colleagues bring order out of masses of data, present the Foundation's findings in readable form, and help analyze the results.

Through every stage of the project, Hinda Greenberg, director of the Foundation's Information Center, gathered the mountains of materials that had to be reviewed for the study. Hinda kept the flow of information going, kept it current, and kept it all together.

I am especially indebted to Louise Underwood, secretary of the Foundation and my assistant, whose daily management of *Basic School* drafts and materials coming across the desk, along with all of the other more routine demands, helped keep the enterprise afloat. Above all, I am grateful for her wisdom, patience, and deep commitment to the Foundation's work.

David Walter, treasurer of the Foundation, must be recognized for his clearheaded counsel and calm management of the financial aspects of Foundation projects, as well as his expertise in overseeing the continuing development of the Foundation's computer network, on which everything now seems to depend. And my thanks go to P. Michael Timpane, who recently joined the Foundation as vice president and senior scholar, for his counsel.

The computer heartbeat of the Foundation is the word processing team. I most especially thank Dawn Ott, supervisor, for her absolute dedication to this project. She gave a thousand percent, and her unflagging energy, her lightning speed, and her sacrifice of many weekends and evenings as the manuscript was being written and edited kept my work moving forward.

Laura Bell also worked extensively in word processing the many drafts throughout the project and has my great thanks. Donna Chiarello recently joined the word processing team and assisted, too, with some of the citation work. I deeply appreciate these colleagues for their fast, efficient work on this and on every other Foundation project.

In administrative work, thanks go to Arlene Hobson Gundrum, assistant treasurer, particularly for her help with the management of seminars and other events hosted by the Foundation. For their secretarial work and other support services, I wish to thank Carol Duryea, Patricia Klensch-Balmer, Kelli-ann Korin Lanino, Robert Lucas, Jacquelyn Minning, Patricia Novak, and Judy Williams. Torin Dilley recently joined us to assist in the Information Center, and has helped with some of the citation work on this project. These colleagues contribute invaluable assistance every single day, keeping Foundation work moving forward.

Finally, I extend my deepest gratitude to Kay, my wife, who, above all others, brought this book to life. She reminded me, early on, that the first years of learning mattered most. Through many hours of lengthy discussion we considered, together, how the Basic School should be shaped. And during the long days and nights of writing, Kay was not only patient and understanding, but even more, she made wonderfully insightful and helpful editorial suggestions and contributed, in the final weeks, endless hours of manuscript review. This project simply could not have been completed without her.

Kay is, in a very real sense, both the inspiration and coauthor of *The Basic School.*

ERNEST L. BOYER
President
The Carnegie Foundation for
the Advancement of Teaching

PREFACE

This book has been in my mind for a long time. I first proposed the Basic School in a 1979 article for the *New York Times*.[1] At that time, I suggested that the first twelve years of formal schooling might be restructured: first, the *Basic School,* where young children would focus in the early years on language and general education; second, the *Common School,* spanning the middle years, devoted to a core of general knowledge; and third, the *Transition School*, with the last two or three years of formal education flexibly arranged, providing students with beginning apprenticeships and collegiate study.

Recently it occurred to me that the *idea* for the Basic School actually goes back even further to the 1960s, when I was chancellor of the State University of New York. Students in those days would declare, in anger, that younger and older people had nothing in common. They challenged the right of the university to require a core of common learning, asking, "What does it mean to be an educated person, anyway?"

Later, during a sabbatical at Cambridge University in England, with a bit of distance from my own world, I reflected on that question, and asked myself, Just what should colleges, as well as schools, be teaching? Is there, in fact, a core of common learning? If so, how should it be defined?

In a very informal way, I started thinking about "common learning," and what it is that all human beings share. What do we all have in common? And would it be possible to organize schools in ways that relate the curriculum even more directly to students' lives, helping them understand more about who they are and, even more important, what we share?

While still in England, I wrote a monograph with Martin Kaplan called *Educating for Survival*, in which we tested, in a very preliminary way, a new approach to education, one in which the curriculum would be organized not on the basis of the disciplines, but around basic human experiences.[2]

In the ensuing years, as U.S. Commissioner of Education, I continued to reflect upon these "human commonalities," and add to them, considering how the idea of shared human experiences might somehow be woven into the fabric of formal education, so the disciplines could be used to illuminate larger, more integrative ends.

Fifteen years ago, I joined The Carnegie Foundation for the Advancement of Teaching, and these questions about both the structure and purposes of education remained in my mind and influenced much of my work.

The first report we published during my tenure was an essay in 1981 called *A Quest for Common Learning: The Aims of General Education*, in which Arthur Levine and I proposed that general education at the college level become more integrated. Colleges, we suggested, should stress "those experiences, relationships, and ethical concerns that are common to all of us simply by virtue of our membership in the human family at a particular moment in history."[3]

In 1983, as a new phase of school reform was about to begin, the Foundation released *High School: A Report on Secondary Education in America*. Here, among other recommendations, we called for a curriculum that would "help all students learn about their human heritage, and the interdependent world in which they live, through a core of common learning based upon those consequential experiences common to all people."[4]

The Foundation returned to higher education in 1987 with the publication of *College: The Undergraduate Experience in America*. Once again, we proposed "a program of general education that introduces students not only to essential knowledge, but also to connections across the disciplines, and, in the end, to the application of knowledge to life beyond the campus." We said: "The integrated core concerns itself with the universal experiences that are common to all people, with those shared activities without which human relationships are diminished and the quality of life reduced."[5]

It was during this project that I became increasingly convinced that education is a seamless web, that one level of learning relates to every other, and that the most promising prospects for educational reform are in the first years of formal learning.

The Carnegie Foundation subsequently embarked on a study that focused on the first ten years of life. We looked at prenatal care, the condition of infants in America, and the needs of preschoolers. In 1991, this study culminated in a report called *Ready to Learn: A Mandate for the Nation,* which outlines the steps we must take, as a nation, to get all children ready for school. We proposed a seven-step strategy: *a healthy start, empowered parents, quality preschool, a responsive workplace, television as teacher, neighborhoods for learning,* and *connections across the generations,* "all of the forces that have such a profound impact on children's lives and shape their readiness to learn." We argued that this agenda is, without question, the right of every child.[6]

But if all children are to be ready for school, surely all schools must be ready for children and, for the last few years, we have devoted literally thousands of hours to a study of elementary education. Our investigation led us down many paths. We examined the research, conducted surveys, and visited schools. We invited educators and early childhood experts to the Foundation. We met with Chief State School Officers, who helped us see how the design of the Basic School would fit into the current political framework and state policies.

Above all, we listened to teachers, who spoke with urgency about how the lives of children have been changing. Children in privileged homes are likely to have had more extensive educational experiences, including the use of technology's latest innovations, while those from impoverished backgrounds are, educationally, still the most neglected. Yet the challenge for school renewal cuts across all social and economic sectors. What is needed, we have concluded, is a new vision of elementary education, a comprehensive plan that makes available, to every child, school practices that really work.

It was at this point in our study that my long interest in an integrated curriculum was stirred again. Young children don't think about categories of knowledge. They follow their curiosity wherever it leads. They are, above all, natural, integrative learners. I concluded that the elementary school, especially, should be organized around a curriculum that is both comprehensive *and* coherent.

As I think about this long journey, I am greatly encouraged by the vitality of the elementary school, by the dedication of principals and teachers, and most especially by their willingness to change. It seems clear to me that the elementary school is the most flexible level of formal learning, a place where the focus is on *children*, not on "the system" or promoting one's career. It was a first-grade teacher in Dayton, Ohio, who sparked my own love affair with language, and it is my deepest hope that *The Basic School* will be of help to the dedicated elementary principals and teachers who each day serve so selflessly our nation's children.

But I am anxious, too. I am concerned that we are not making sufficient progress in our effort to improve the nation's schools. I am concerned, as well, about a loss of confidence in this country not just in school reform, but in the very idea of public education. I'm troubled when I hear the nation's schools referred to as a "failed system." I see no way for America's future to be secure without a quality education for *every* child, not just the most advantaged.

The lives of our children and the health of the schools they attend transcend political boundaries, and I remain convinced that in our search for excellence, it *is* possible to find common ground, for the sake of children. In the end, this is what the Basic School is all about.

One hundred and twelve years ago, Sitting Bull, a Lakota Sioux, said: "Let us put our minds together and see what life we can make for our children."[7] Standing on the threshold of a new millennium, we have an opportunity to bring a renewed commitment to America's most essential educational institution—the elementary school. Nothing is more important.

The Vision of the Basic School

- *The School as Community*
- *The Principal and Teachers as Leaders*
- *Parents as Partners*
- *The Centrality of Language*
- *A Curriculum with Coherence*
- *Measuring for Success*
- *A Climate for Active Learning*
- *Resources to Enrich*
- *Support Services for Children*
- *A Commitment to Character*

PROLOGUE: A NEW BEGINNING

Prologue: A New Beginning

We propose, in this report, a new place for learning called The Basic School. The Basic School is not so much an *institution* as it is an *idea*, one that is, we believe, appropriate for every elementary school.

We call this school "basic," first of all, because it takes the push for school renewal back to the beginning, to the first years of formal learning, and back to each local school, where, without question, all teaching and learning must occur. It's "basic" because it gives priority to language and proposes a curriculum with coherence. Finally, the school we describe is "basic" because it identifies the proven components of an effective education and brings them all together in a single institution—the Basic School.

Last fall, more than three million kindergarten children[1] enrolled in over fifty thousand public and private schools from Bangor, Maine, to the islands of Hawaii.[2] Most of these young students arrived at school anxious, but also eager. Some were cheerful, others troubled. Some skipped and ran, others could not walk. This new generation of students came from countless neighborhoods, from a great diversity of cultures, speaking more languages than most of us could name. And the challenge we now face is to ensure that every child will become a confident, resourceful learner.

Children are, of course, *always* learning. They learn as they touch the earth, feel the grass, dig into the sand. Children learn as they chase pigeons in the park, study drifting clouds, and watch ants scurrying across city sidewalks. "The child is the most avid learner of all living things on this earth," as Ashley Montagu observed.[3] Yet, this marvelous gift of continuous discovery can be diminished or enhanced. And the purpose of the Basic School is to keep the urge to learn alive in every child.

For years, America has been working hard to improve the nation's schools and reform has been high on the public agenda. As a result, academic standards have been raised, teacher certification requirements have been tightened, and educational innovations have been introduced from coast to coast. Without question, progress has been made.

Today, America's best schools are, we believe, among the most outstanding in the world. Others are succeeding, often under difficult conditions. But it's also true that far too many schools are only marginal at best, and that some, often those in our most troubled neighborhoods, should hardly be called schools, as U.S. secretary of education Richard W. Riley put it.[4] In one suburban elementary school in Ohio, a fourth-grade teacher told us: "We seem to be working harder, with fewer gains."[5]

When we asked elementary school teachers in a national survey how the quality of American education today compares to five years ago, more than 40 percent said "about the same." Thirty-two percent said it's gotten worse. Only 26 percent said it's better. Parents, we discovered, were even more pessimistic about the progress being made. Twenty percent felt the quality of education is better. Forty percent stated it is about the same. But forty percent said it's worse, compared to five years ago (table 1). School success, ultimately, must be measured by student performance, not opinion polls. Still, no one can be fully satisfied with where we are today.

We reach one incontrovertible conclusion. The world has changed and schools must change, too. The lives of children who enroll in school today will span a new century. Those who graduate will enter what Peter F. Drucker calls "the knowledge society"[6] which requires higher literacy, more technical competence, and lifelong learning. Knowledge has, without question, become our most precious resource. And if, in the days ahead, educators cannot help students become literate and well informed, if the coming generation cannot be helped to see well beyond the confines of their own lives, the nation's prospects for the future will be dangerously diminished.

Clearly, the push for school renewal needs a new beginning. This time the focus must be on the early years, on *elementary* education. Every level of learning is important. No sector should be neglected. But school failure starts very early, and if all children do not have a good beginning, if they do not receive the support and encouragement needed during the first years of life, it will be difficult, if not impossible, to compensate fully for the failure later on.

A third-grade teacher in Wyoming stated the case this way: "With all the talk about school renewal, there is a tendency to overlook elementary schools. The first years must be recognized as the most essential. Until the elementary school becomes a priority for renewal, education in this country will not make much improvement."

TABLE 1

HOW DOES THE QUALITY OF EDUCATION IN THE NATION TODAY
COMPARE WITH FIVE YEARS AGO?

	PERCENTAGE AGREEING	
	TEACHERS	PARENTS
Better	26%	20%
About the same	42	40
Worse	32	40

SOURCE: The Carnegie Foundation for the Advancement of Teaching and the George
H. Gallup International Institute, The International Schooling Project, 1994
(United States).

Responding to this challenge, The Carnegie Foundation for the
Advancement of Teaching launched, several years ago, a study of
the elementary school. We searched the literature, consulted
scholars, conducted national and international surveys, and sent
researchers into schools all across the country.

During these visits, we were struck, time and time again, by the
commitment of principals, the eagerness of students, the concern
of parents, and most especially by the dedication of teachers, who
are, we concluded, the unsung heroes of the nation. Above all, we
were impressed by the way so many of the nation's elementary
schools have adjusted dramatically to new demands. We conclude that the elementary school is, as former U.S. secretary of
education William J. Bennett put it, a place of hope.[7]

Still, this is not the time to be complacent.

We were troubled, for example, that teachers in the elementary
schools have little time to work together and that many parents

are not actively engaged in the education of their children. We were troubled, too, by the confusion over what schools should teach and how students should be assessed, issues that go to the very heart of quality education. We also became concerned that a rigid class schedule and poor resources often restrict learning, especially for the least advantaged. Finally, at the very time the nation's children need ethical and moral guidance, we found schools perplexed about what virtues they should, in fact, be teaching.

We are convinced that a new vision of elementary education is urgently required, one that presents a comprehensive, practical plan of action based on best practices that would be appropriate for every school. We agree with James Rodenmayer, the principal at Etna Road Elementary School in Whitehall, Ohio, who said to us: "There is a growing urgency all over the country about the direction of education and a sense that, nationwide, we must do better, for the sake of our children."

How, then, should we proceed?

The plan we present in this report is not just another "pilot project." It is not yet one more novel "experiment." Rather, what we have done is to identify practices that really work and put them all together in what we call the Basic School. The piecemeal approach to school reform has been tried. During the past decade, we have had literally hundreds of isolated innovations. What's needed now is a comprehensive approach to school renewal, one that pulls together the essential elements of quality education and makes them available to every child.

After completing our research, we concluded that the most essential ingredient of a successful school—the one idea that holds it all together—is best described by the simple word "connections." An effective school connects people, to create *community*. An effective school connects the curriculum, to achieve *coherence*. An effective school connects classrooms and resources, to enrich the learning *climate*. And an effective school connects learning to life, to build *character*.

These four priorities—*community, curriculum coherence, climate*, and *character*—are the building blocks for the Basic School. Fitted within each of these priorities are specific proposals— programs that, we discovered, really work. The goal of the Basic School is to present an overall strategy for renewal, one that seems to fit all institutions while, at the same time, encouraging every school to develop, within this overarching framework, its own distinctive program.

FIRST: THE SCHOOL AS COMMUNITY

·   *A Shared Vision*. The Basic School has, as the first requirement, a clear and vital mission. The school is a place where everyone comes together to promote learning. Every classroom is, itself, a community. But in the Basic School, the separate classrooms are connected by a sense of *purpose*, in a climate that is *communicative, just, disciplined*, and *caring*, with occasions for *celebration*.

·   *Teachers as Leaders*. In the Basic School, teachers are empowered. Working together as teams, they serve as mentors to their students and have the time and resources needed to be professionally renewed. The

principal in the Basic School is *lead* teacher, the one
who guides the institution more by inspiration than
directive.

·   *Parents as Partners*. In the Basic School, the circle of
community extends outward to embrace parents, who
are viewed as the child's first and most important
teachers. A vital partnership is created between the
home and school, one that begins during the preschool years, is strengthened when the child formally
enrolls, and continues from kindergarten through grade
five.

SECOND: A CURRICULUM WITH COHERENCE

·   *The Centrality of Language*. In the Basic School,
literacy is the first and most essential goal. All children are expected to become proficient in the written
and spoken word. But language in this school is defined broadly to include words, numbers, and the arts,
the essential tools of learning which, taken together,
help create a curriculum with coherence.

·   *The Core Commonalities*. In the Basic School, all
students become well informed. They study the various fields of knowledge, which are organized, thematically, within a framework called "the Core
Commonalities." These eight commonalities, based
on shared human experiences, integrate the traditional subjects, helping students see connections across
the disciplines and relate what they learn to life.

·   *Measuring Results.* The Basic School is accountable to parents, to students, and to the community at large. Academic standards are established both in language and the Core Commonalities, with benchmarks to monitor student achievement. The personal and social qualities of students also are observed and evaluated informally by teachers. Assessment in the Basic School is, always, in the service of learning.

THIRD: A CLIMATE FOR LEARNING

·   *Patterns to Fit Purpose.* In the Basic School, every student is encouraged to become a disciplined, creative, well-motivated learner. Class size is kept small, the teaching schedule is flexible, and student grouping arrangements are varied to promote learning. Connections are made across the generations, to strengthen community and enrich the lives of students.

·   *Resources to Enrich.* The Basic School makes available to all students rich resources for learning, from building blocks to books. Libraries, zoos, museums, and parks in the surrounding community become resources, too. And on the threshold of a new century, the Basic School gives students access to the new electronic tools that connect each classroom to vast networks of knowledge.

·   *Services for Children.* The Basic School is committed to serving the whole child, acknowledging that a student's physical, social, and emotional well-being also relates to learning. Beyond a solid academic program, the school provides basic health and counseling services for students, referrals for families, and a new calendar and clock, with after-school and summer enrichment programs for learning and creative play.

FOURTH: A COMMITMENT TO CHARACTER

· *The Core Virtues*. The Basic School is concerned with the ethical and moral dimensions of a child's life. The goal is to assure that all students, on leaving school, will have developed a keen sense of personal and civic responsibility. Seven core virtues, such as respect, compassion, and perseverance, are emphasized to guide the Basic School as it promotes excellence in living, as well as learning.

· *Living with Purpose*. The core virtues of the Basic School are taught both by word and deed. Through the curriculum, through school climate, and through service, students are encouraged to apply the lessons of the classroom to the world around them.

These, then, are the four priorities of the Basic School. The first priority, *community*, focuses on how people relate to one another. The second priority, *curriculum coherence*, considers what all students should learn. The third priority, *climate*, deals with effective teaching and learning. The fourth priority, *character*, considers how the school experience shapes the ethical and moral lives of children.

Many proposals presented in this report are already being practiced, to one degree or another, in schools from coast to coast. What we suggest, however, is to bring them all together in one place, encouraging every elementary school to implement the plan in its own distinctive way.

In our search for excellence in education, a large, inspired vision is required, and national goals can surely give direction to the effort. But when all is said and done, school renewal must occur at the local level in every school. And it is our hope that this report will be helpful to principals and teachers all across the country who are working so diligently to educate the nation's children.

Again, this vision we call the Basic School is "basic" because, *organizationally*, it proposes a grassroots approach to education reform. It's basic, *educationally*, by affirming the early years of learning. It is basic, *pedagogically*, in providing a curriculum with coherence. And it's basic, *strategically*, in embracing proven practices that work.

Ultimately, the aim of the Basic School is not just to build a better school, but, above all, to build a better world for children. It is our deepest hope that not a single child, let alone a whole generation of children, should pass through the schoolhouse door unprepared for the world that lies before them. And there is, we believe, an urgency to this effort. Chilean poet Gabriela Mistral wrote: "Many things we need can wait. The child cannot. Now is the time his bones are being formed, his blood is being made, his mind is being developed. To him we cannot say tomorrow, his name is today."[8]

Responding to this challenge is, in the end, what the Basic School is all about.

THE SCHOOL AS COMMUNITY

A Shared Vision

> *The Basic School has, as the first requirement, a clear and vital mission. The school is a place where everyone comes together to promote learning. Every classroom is, itself, a community. But in the Basic School, the separate classrooms are connected by a sense of* purpose, *in a climate that is* communicative, just, disciplined, *and* caring, *with occasions for* celebration.

The Basic School is, above all else, a *community for learning*, a place where staff and students, along with parents, have a shared vision of what the institution is seeking to accomplish. There is simply no way to achieve educational excellence in a school where purposes are blurred, where teachers and students fail to communicate thoughtfully with each other, and where parents are uninvolved in the education of their children. Community is, without question, the glue that holds an effective school together.[1]

As we entered Jackson-Keller Elementary School in San Antonio, Texas, a parent greeted us at the door. Second-graders, leaving on a field trip, cheerfully waved goodbye. Walking down colorful corridors, we passed one classroom where third-graders were planting seeds. Next door, a team of teachers from different grades worked together on a new lesson plan. As we moved along, the principal, Alicia Thomas, hugged children, greeted teachers, and occasionally paused to talk with parents. We passed two girls holding hands—a fifth-grader and a first-grader—who were, Mrs. Thomas told us, part of the school's "buddy" system, which "helps us build community," she observed.[2]

Organizationally, the Basic School starts with kindergarten. At the upper end, there is no rigid breakpoint. Some may run through grade four, others grade six. We suggest grade five, for several reasons. First, ten-year-olds, who typically are not yet in puberty, often are more comfortable with younger children than with teenagers. Also, by staying with younger students, fifth-graders can have a "capstone experience" in their final year, tutoring and caring for others, applying what they've learned, becoming, themselves, confident community leaders.

The spirit of community in the Basic School requires first "a sense of place"—a facility that is functional and aesthetically appealing.[3] Many schools we visited were built years ago, and it's really troubling that while we've built glitzy banks and shopping malls, the school facilities are, in far too many neighborhoods, shockingly neglected. Still, even old buildings can become comfortable and inviting. And we were struck, time and time again, by the way creative teachers can transform barren corridors and dreary cinder block classrooms into visually inviting and educationally exciting places.

School size matters, too.[4] "If all the research on the best environments in which to . . . educate children could be boiled down to three words, they would be Small Is Beautiful," notes educator

Winifred Gallagher.[5] Small institutions encourage *community*. And while no arbitrary line is drawn, we suggest, as a rule of thumb, that the Basic School be small enough for everyone to be known by name—perhaps with no more than four to five hundred students.[6] Larger schools might be organized as schools within a school.

The Nelson County School District, in the foothills of Virginia's Blue Ridge Mountains, discovered just how closely school size relates to learning. District leaders were about to close a rural school, but local citizens fought the consolidation plan, arguing that no other school would work as well. After interviewing students, teachers, staff members, and parents, the consultants concluded: "A school that works is a place that welcomes people, a place where everyone is known by name. Rather than being 'institutional' in character, it looks and feels like 'home.'"[7]

But *community* doesn't just happen, even in a small school.[8] To become a true community, the institution must be organized around people, "around relationships and ideas," as Trinity University professor Thomas J. Sergiovanni puts it.[9] Communities, he says, "create social structures that bond people together in a oneness, and that bind them to a set of shared values and ideas."

What we are really talking about is the *culture* of the school, the vision that is shared, the way people relate to one another. And during school visits, we discovered six essential qualities of human interaction that seem to move a school from fragmentation to a vital place for learning.

Simply stated, a school becomes a *community for learning* when it is:

- · a *purposeful* place,
- · a *communicative* place,
- · a *just* place,
- · a *disciplined* place,
- · a *caring* place, and
- · a *celebrative* place.

These key conditions, when embraced by everyone at the school and lived out each day, create the kind of community for learning that every Basic School should strive to be.

A PURPOSEFUL PLACE

A school community is, first, a *purposeful* place, with a clear and vital mission. Research reveals that when school purposes are well defined and energetically pursued, student performance will improve.[10]

A Rand Corporation study found that students are most successful in schools where the principal, parents, teachers, and students pull together to achieve a common cause, and where everyone accepts responsibility to ensure that the shared educational goals will be met. In the most effective schools, there is a social contract that staff and students accept as they join the school community.[11]

The shared vision of the Basic School is *excellence for all*. The school affirms, as its central mission, that every child has a right to a quality education, that high academic standards must be set, and that every child can and will succeed in ways that reflect his or her own unique aptitudes and interests. This vision defines the purpose of the Basic School and becomes, for both teachers and students, the source of daily inspiration.[12]

At the Willard Model School in Norfolk, Virginia, students and staff pause, each morning, to recite this pledge: "I believe that I can be a good student. I believe that I can achieve. I believe that if I work hard I will succeed. Therefore, I will work hard each day to do my best. I can learn. I will learn."

Beyond "excellence for all," the Basic School defines five sharply focused *goals*, which are, we believe, appropriate for every elementary school. These goals, which focus on the whole child—the educational, social, emotional, physical, and moral needs of children —give day-to-day purpose and direction to the school. They are:

·   *First, to communicate effectively.* In the Basic School, language is not just another subject; it's the means by which all other subjects are pursued. All students in the school are expected to read with comprehension, and to write with clarity using standard English. They learn to speak and listen effectively, accurately compute, and engage creatively in the arts. The goal is literacy for all.

·   *Second, to acquire a core of essential knowledge.* All Basic School students become well informed. They learn about the world through a study of history, science, literature, civics, and other traditional academic subjects. The educational focus of the Basic School is, however, not just on *content*, but on *context*. Beyond a core of knowledge, students make connections across disciplines and, through an integrated curriculum, relate what they learn to life. The goal is to help all students gain both knowledge and perspective.

·   *Third, to be a disciplined, motivated learner.* Students in the Basic School learn to gather and evaluate information, solve problems, and develop the skills needed to study on their own. Teachers in the school serve as mentors to students and make available to them resources to enrich their education. The goal is to encourage students to remain curious and become active, self-directed learners.

·   *Fourth, to have a sense of well-being.* The focus of the Basic School is on the *whole* child. The school acknowledges that every student has special aptitudes and interests, as well as special needs, and that when it comes to learning, mind and body cannot be divided. The goal is to give all children the support they need to be physically healthy, socially confident, and emotionally secure.

·   *Fifth, to live responsibly.* In the Basic School, there is a commitment to good character. The school accepts its obligation to teach, by word and deed, those core virtues that promote good conduct and good citizenship. The goal is to assure that each student becomes an ethically responsible person.

The Basic School, with a shared vision and clearly defined goals, is a purposeful place.

A COMMUNICATIVE PLACE

The Basic School is a *communicative* place where the emphasis is on the integrity of ideas, not the authority of an office. The climate is collegial. Everyone in the school speaks and listens carefully to each other, creating a relationship of trust among the principal, teachers, students, and parents. At Laurel Ridge Elementary School in Fairfax, Virginia, the motto reads: "Kindness is *spoken* here."

During one school visit, we noticed a second-grade teacher asking a third-grade teacher about a troubled child she'd had the year before. Down the hall, a first-grader was listening attentively as his teacher explained why students aren't allowed to go to the playground alone. Later in the day, the principal dropped by the teachers' lounge to visit with a newly recruited colleague. These quiet exchanges, which should go on continuously in schools, involved openness and honesty, accompanied by respect.

In the Basic School, the conversation between teachers and students is, always, a two-way street. Students feel free to express their own ideas. There is, throughout the school, less emphasis on communicating "through channels" and more attention given to openness. Each classroom is, itself, a community where teachers become listeners and learners, too. A third-grade teacher in the Midwest told us: "Almost every day I learn something from my students. Sometimes it's a surprising fact, but more often it's an insight or a truly provocative question. But to learn, I first must listen."

In the end, what matters most in the Basic School is not the amount of talk, but the *quality* of the communication. Wayne

Booth, of the University of Chicago, reminds us that, all too often, our attempts to speak and listen seem to be vicious circles, spiraling downward. But he concludes that channels of communication can, in fact, be directed upward. "[W]e have all experienced moments," he wrote, "when the spiral moved upward, when one party's effort to listen and speak just a little bit better, produced a similar response, making it possible to try a bit harder—and on up the spiral to moments of genuine understanding."[13]

The Basic School is a communicative place, one filled with moments of genuine understanding.

A JUST PLACE

The Basic School is a *just* place where everyone—the principal, teachers, and students—are respectful of each other. There is, in the school, a feeling of fair play, a widely shared belief that everyone, regardless of race or gender,[14] will have an equal opportunity to succeed. No community can be sustained in an environment where justice is denied.

Young children have an almost intuitive sense of fairness. They expect justice, and during school visits, we occasionally heard students on the playground declare firmly, "That's not fair!" School conflicts, we observed, frequently were sparked by the feeling that someone was getting special favors, and while adults may not voice their concern quite so bluntly, this same sense of fairness is, for grownups, never far below the surface.

Clearly, a school, to be a truly effective community, must be a *just* place. Yet our research revealed that elementary school students, like many adults, are inclined to make prejudicial judgments. Many believe, for example, that girls are better than boys at "writing reports or stories," "playing a musical instrument," and "acting in plays." Boys, on the other hand, are thought to be better at "playing sports" and "doing a science experiment" (table 2). Both students and teachers should be encouraged to talk about why such stereotypes exist.

In the Basic School, the commitment to justice is socially *and* educationally affirmed. The school rejects, absolutely, any separation of students into "winners" and "losers." There is no rigid "tracking." Rather, students are grouped in a variety of ways, to accommodate a variety of goals. High expectations for *both* boys and girls are set, and resources for learning—books, computers, art supplies—are divided equitably among students and across grade levels.

In affirming justice, the Basic School is especially attentive to the growing racial and ethnic diversity in our culture. Today, the face of young America is changing. By the year 2000, more than one-third of the students in the nation's schools will be African-American, Asian, or Hispanic. In many schools, students from these backgrounds already are the majority.[15] And the Basic School celebrates this rich tapestry of talent. As a just community, the school promotes equality of opportunity, and students from every racial, ethnic, and religious background are warmly welcomed.

The Basic School is a just place where, as one teacher put it, "everyone is special."

TABLE 2

WHO DOES BETTER AT EACH OF THESE ACTIVITIES?
(PERCENTAGE OF STUDENTS AGREEING)

	BOTH THE SAME	GIRLS BETTER	BOYS BETTER
Solving math problems	74%	12%	14%
Doing a science experiment	68	8	24
Writing reports or stories	61	33	6
Acting in plays	60	36	4
Drawing and painting	58	29	14
Playing a musical instrument	57	33	10
Speaking in class	52	25	23
Playing sports/gym	40	2	58

SOURCE: The Carnegie Foundation for the Advancement of Teaching and the George H. Gallup International Institute, The International Schooling Project, 1994 (United States).

A DISCIPLINED PLACE

The Basic School is a *disciplined* place. All students in the school discover very early that individual rights must be balanced by responsibility to the group.[16] It is simply impossible to sustain community in a chaotic climate, where student conduct is undisciplined and where children fail to live by fairly imposed rules. Child psychologist David Elkind puts the challenge this way: "Children need a sense that somebody cares enough to protect them. To provide that sense, we must become adults to our kids."[17]

Most elementary schools are, we discovered, safe and cordial places. However, we also observed that the lack of civility that saturates the world of children outside the school spills over into classrooms and flares up on playgrounds.[18]

During lunch break at a midsized suburban school, one seasoned fourth-grade teacher observed: "Every year more and more of my time is spent with discipline. I spend a lot of time teaching cooperation and courtesy. The ability of children to play together without fighting has decreased." A third-grade teacher in Minnesota said: "I see lots of disturbing conduct which seems to be growing even among the younger students. But today's children are simply imitating the violence they see in the adult world."

Students, themselves, report problems among peers. When we asked nine- to eleven-year-olds about student conduct at their school, more than half said "fighting" and "bullying" are serious problems. More than a third said "stealing" is a serious problem, and 13 percent identified "carrying weapons such as knives" as a serious problem at their school (table 3).

Children, like the rest of us, work best when they feel safe, when reasonable rules are sensitively established, thoughtfully explained, and fairly enforced. Further, research reveals that academic achievement demonstrably improves in schools where students feel safe.[19] The Basic School, as a disciplined place, has a code of conduct which students themselves help define.[20] Standards of kindness, punctuality, and courtesy are modeled and taught in the classroom every day.

A fourth-grade teacher in Rochester, New York, explained to us how he establishes classroom rules and why he believes the children respond so well to the sense of discipline this creates. "The kids know what to expect," he said. "It helps them have a strong sense of identity, and builds community. Some of my students live such peripatetic lives. They move, and family relationships change and, for them, it's nice if a teacher can be a rock. Or if your mom just went to jail or your father just left, you can come to class and find a little stability, a little bit of peace."

TABLE 3

WHICH OF THESE ARE SERIOUS PROBLEMS IN YOUR SCHOOL?

	PERCENTAGE OF STUDENTS RESPONDING "YES"
Students fighting with each other	56%
Students bullying or picking on each other	54
Stealing	38
Students carrying weapons such as knives	13

SOURCE: The Carnegie Foundation for the Advancement of Teaching and the George H. Gallup International Institute, The International Schooling Project, 1994 (United States).

Life is a balance of freedom and constraints, and students in the Basic School begin to understand that everyone lives within limits, that, along with freedom, the rights of others must be sensitively respected. The goal is not to have a list of unenforceable commandments. Rather, it is to assure that all parts of school life are governed by high standards.

The Basic School is a disciplined place.

A CARING PLACE

In building community, the Basic School is also a *caring* place, where the principal, teachers, and students are respectfully attentive to each other. In a world of hard-edged competition, the term "caring" may sound soft, even sentimental. However, everyone needs to be loved and continuously affirmed, from birth to the very end. Biologist Mary E. Clark reminds us that social embeddedness is the essence of our nature. "Human beings," she said, "have an absolute need for social intercourse from the first moments of life."[21]

Children, especially, have a deep, abiding urge to feel that they belong. James P. Comer, child psychiatrist at Yale University and highly respected authority on children, insists that education cannot be isolated from the emotional needs of children, asserting that: "[Y]ou've got to provide an environment that allows children to feel wanted, valued, and accepted, one that allows them to accept you."[22] Yet, the sad truth is that far too many youngsters in this country are lonely,[23] neglected, even threatened.

In one Carnegie Foundation survey, we found that about 30 percent of elementary school students go home every afternoon to an empty house (see table 27).[24] In another survey, about one in three say they "worry a lot." And one-fourth report they are afraid of "being threatened or attacked in their own neighborhood" (table 4). It's clear that, for many children, their confidence and sense of well-being are often undermined, both in and outside school.

During a hurried lunch break at a large, inner-city elementary school, we talked with teachers about *caring*. "How is it possible to create such a climate?" we wanted to know. One fifth-grade teacher responded: "I emphasize to kids that you can do positive things in groups. I work with the whole 'gang' concept, that there are good gangs and bad gangs. I stress the positive side of groups, one in which kids learn to care about each other. Children in this school live in tough neighborhoods. They need to feel that we can get through this together. I have tried planting a seed of hope, to let them know someone really cares."

TABLE 4

WHICH OF THESE DESCRIBE YOU OR YOUR SCHOOL?

	PERCENTAGE OF STUDENTS RESPONDING "YES"
Students often feel afraid that they will be punished at my school.	35%
I worry a lot.	31
I am afraid of being threatened or attacked in my own neighborhood.	26

SOURCE: The Carnegie Foundation for the Advancement of Teaching and the George H. Gallup International Institute, The International Schooling Project, 1994 (United States).

In the Basic School, teachers and students reach out to others. There is, in the school, a "buddy" system that matches children across grade levels, providing a climate of caring and support. Eunice Kennedy Shriver, who for years has promoted the vision of a community of caring, declared: "Our children need to be taught, both at home and in school, the importance of caring, responsibility, respect, trust, and family in a time when these values need tremendous reinforcement. Our children need to know that these same values have meaning and relevance in the world which they face every day—in their families, their classrooms, their communities."[25]

The Basic School is a caring place.

A CELEBRATIVE PLACE

Finally, the Basic School, as a community, is a *celebrative* place. Families celebrate, nations celebrate, and, surely, schools must pause to celebrate[26]—beginning first day of school. Rather than "drop" their children off, parents, grandparents, and guardians are welcomed into the Basic School, joining with teachers, students, and staff for both remembrance and anticipation.

At the Dick School in Philadelphia, parents and students gathered, the first day of school, on the playground. Soon everyone was invited into the colorfully decorated assembly hall. Nilsa Gonzalez, the principal, welcomed everyone and introduced the staff, including the custodian and secretaries. Returning students welcomed newcomers. School purposes were discussed and plans for the coming year carefully explained. Everyone asked lots of questions. Many parents stayed all day, meeting with their children's teachers, sharing experiences with one another. "At the end of the day, I was giving everyone hugs," Ms. Gonzalez reported. "And I was still giving hugs the second day."

It was a moment of celebration.

In the end, the Basic School is an institution held together by something far more than connecting corridors and a common schedule. It is a community for learning with a *shared purpose, good communication*, and a climate with *justice, discipline, caring*, and occasions for *celebration.*

These characteristics of community cannot be taken for granted. They must be continuously nurtured, and occasionally monitored, as well. Specifically, we recommend that, at least once a year, the Basic School pause to evaluate itself, asking everyone to respond to questions such as these: Does this school have shared educational goals? Do we speak and listen carefully to each other? Is everyone at our school treated fairly? Do we have reasonable rules that are well known and sensitively enforced?

What evidence do we have that this is a caring place? Do we have occasions for celebration? Which school activities strengthen these qualities, and which restrict them?

Community is, then, the first priority of the Basic School. "You have to have community before anything else," is the way Patricia Bolaños, principal at the Key School in Indianapolis, puts it. And as elementary schools become more strongly unified, within themselves, it seems reasonable to expect that this spirit of community will extend well beyond the school, bringing neighborhoods together.

Author Alex Kotlowitz put the challenge this way: "We need to rebuild a sense of community because our greatest hope lies with our children. And the place to begin is in our schools. We need to use the school as a building block to rebuilding community at large. And the elementary school is the one remaining institution that is dedicated to children."[27]

Building community is *the first priority* of the Basic School.

Teachers as Leaders

> *In the Basic School, teachers are empowered. Working together as teams, they serve as mentors to their students and have the time and resources needed to be professionally renewed. The principal in the Basic School is* lead *teacher, the one who guides the institution more by inspiration than directive.*

In the Basic School, community begins with a shared vision. It's sustained by teachers who, as school leaders, bring inspiration and direction to the institution. Who, after all, knows more about the classroom? Who is better able to inspire children? Who can evaluate, more sensitively, the educational progress of each student? And who but teachers create a true community for learning? Teachers are, without question, the heartbeat of a successful school.

Research on effective schools also cites the principal as essential.[1] And in the Basic School, the principal is viewed as *lead* teacher, the one who guides the institution more by inspiration than directive and, like a symphony conductor, brings the school together in melodic ways.[2] One principal with whom we spoke captured this spirit of leadership when she said: "The key to building a successful school is to move away from the traditional 'principal-staff' role and create in the school a feeling of *community*."

31

Former U.S. commissioner of education Harold Howe II, in commenting on the essential relationship between the principal and teachers, made this observation: "If I had to pick out one set of heroes and heroines in the current school reform movement . . . I would be frustrated by having to choose between two groups: those teachers who have managed to change their classrooms into places where their students can find excitement about learning . . . and those principals who have developed the personal skills to encourage and help teachers to reach for such classrooms amidst all the cacophony of school reform."[3]

Teachers with whom we spoke occasionally criticized the principal at their school for lack of vision. Most often, however, they expressed appreciation for the support and encouragement they received. Further, our national survey revealed that more than 70 percent of the teachers in this country rated their principal's support for teachers as "excellent" or "good." Sixty-seven percent rated the principal's "overall performance" high. Nearly two-thirds gave high marks to principals for their "treatment of teachers as partners" (table 5). One fifth-grade teacher told us: "I feel that the one thing that makes our school succeed is the principal, who continuously reminds us why we're here."

Lillian Brinkley, principal of the Willard Model School in Norfolk, Virginia, describes her role this way: "I believe leadership is the ability to inspire others. I don't ask teachers to do anything I wouldn't do. Every teacher is a leader at this school. When teachers have ownership, they give their best and see to it that their project succeeds." Willard has faculty meetings every Thursday for one hour while paraprofessionals work with students. And principal Brinkley ends every staff meeting with a discussion

TABLE 5

PLEASE EVALUATE THE PRINCIPAL IN YOUR SCHOOL IN
RELATION TO EACH OF THE FOLLOWING
ATTITUDES OR ACTIVITIES.

	PERCENTAGE OF TEACHERS RESPONDING "EXCELLENT" OR "GOOD"
Support for teachers	71%
Overall performance	67
Treatment of teachers as partners	62

SOURCE: The Carnegie Foundation for the Advancement of Teaching, National Survey of Public School Teachers, 1987.

about dreams. She asks each teacher, "What wishes do you have for yourselves? What dreams do you have for your students?"[4]

If teachers are to lead, if their dreams are to be fulfilled, they themselves must be empowered. The reality is, however, that far too many teachers are not involved in important school decisions. They are assigned lots of accountability, but with little authority to act.[5] And it's sad but true that with all the talk about "school-based management," the principal and teachers at many schools are still able to make only "marginal changes," according to Stanford University professor Michael W. Kirst.[6]

Consider, for example, that only one-third of the teachers in this country feel they have "considerable influence" in determining the discipline policy and in establishing curriculum at their school, according to a recent U.S. Department of Education survey. Even fewer say they can shape their own inservice education programs, and just 27 percent feel they have "considerable influence" over

TABLE 6

AT THIS SCHOOL, HOW MUCH INFLUENCE DO YOU THINK
TEACHERS HAVE OVER SCHOOL POLICY IN THESE AREAS?

	PERCENTAGE OF TEACHERS RESPONDING "CONSIDERABLE INFLUENCE"
Determining discipline policy	37%
Establishing curriculum	35
Determining content of inservice programs	33
Setting policy on grouping students in classes by ability	27

SOURCE: Judith Anderson, "Who's In Charge? Teachers' Views on Control Over School Policy and Classroom Practices," *Research Report*, U.S. Department of Education, Office of Educational Research and Improvement, August 1994; percentage of public school teachers responding 5 or 6 on a 6-point scale of agreement, with 5 and 6 indicating "considerable influence."

how students in their school should be "grouped" (table 6). One teacher told us: "I'm constantly being told that I should lead, and yet I'm spending more and more time just filling out the forms."

Excellence in education cannot be externally imposed. And the time has come to abandon the top-down approach to educational renewal. Leadership, ultimately, must be school-based. "There is no educating of young people in the school 'system,'" John Goodlad reminds us. "It all takes place in tens of thousands of individual schools."[7]

In the Basic School, the governing board should be freed from unnecessary mandates. Guided by national goals and statewide standards, each local board should have the authority to act. The

board, in turn, after defining the school's mission and key policies, should then place confidence in the principal and teachers to
lead, holding them accountable for *outcomes*, not day-to-day
procedures.

TEACHERS AS TEAM MEMBERS

Once empowered, teachers in the Basic School work together as
team members. They view the *whole* school, not just their own
classroom, as the place for learning. Research reveals that the
most successful learning does, in fact, occur in schools where
teachers not only teach skillfully in separate classrooms, but also
find solutions *together*.[8] Robert Spillane, superintendent of Fairfax
County Public Schools in Virginia, makes the point: "All of the
current thinking and research on good teaching practices and
effective schools point to the importance of collegiality among
teachers."[9]

Teachers, we discovered, actually prefer to work in groups. For
example, when we asked elementary teachers, nationwide, about
curriculum planning, they expressed strongest preference for
"groups of teachers working together." Only 5 percent supported
the idea of each teacher working alone (table 7). One fifth-grade
teacher said: "After years of working in isolation, I recently
became part of a four-teacher team. As a result, I find my enjoy-
ment has greatly increased, my teaching has become more effective, and students are learning more."

The key to team planning, of course, is *time*.[10] Yet time is
precisely what most teachers do not have.[11] A second-grade
teacher in a Midwest school observed, with a touch of sadness:

TABLE 7

WHO DO YOU THINK BEST CONTROLS
THE CONTENT OF THE SCHOOL CURRICULUM?

	PERCENTAGE OF TEACHERS AGREEING
Groups of teachers working together	40%
State officials	27
Local authorities	27
Each teacher working alone on his/her own	5
National officials	1

SOURCE: The Carnegie Foundation for the Advancement of Teaching and the George H. Gallup International Institute, *The International Schooling Project*, 1994 (United States).

"We are so busy *doing*, that, quite literally, we have no time for *planning*." Another teacher told us: "Days, even weeks, go by and I am unable to have a serious, professional conversation with any of my colleagues in the school."

Typically, elementary school teachers begin instruction with the first bell in the morning.[12] They are still with children to the last bell in the afternoon, "with hardly time for rest stops," one teacher said. There is, of course, the brief lunch break, and perhaps a hurried recess, but even then teachers often are "on duty," supervising students.[13] Gene I. Maeroff, in his insightful study *The Empowerment of Teachers*, summarized the problem this way: "The way that schools are structured seems to conspire against collegiality and the empowerment it can produce."[14]

Consider, for example, that 41 percent of elementary school teachers in this country say they "seldom" or "never" meet with other teachers for planning and preparation, according to our survey. Only 17 percent say they meet "frequently" with other teachers. In contrast, just 16 percent of Japanese teachers say they "seldom" or "never" meet with colleagues (table 8).

Paul A. Gagnon, professor at Boston University, tells of meeting with a group of teachers in an affluent, suburban school district to talk about the history curriculum. "Many of them," he said, "had not seen, much less spoken to, their colleagues for weeks! And all of them said that they never have the time to sit down and talk about subject matter and each other's teaching of it." Professor Gagnon asks: "How *could* they be expected to work together on anything so complicated as a K-12 curriculum?"[15]

In the Basic School, teachers, as team members, have shared goals, and time is regularly set aside for professional collaboration. Specifically we recommend that teachers in the school meet for several days at the beginning and end of each school year, and preferably get together at least once a week.[16] Bringing teachers together is, we recognize, easier said than done, yet many schools are, in fact, finding ways to do it.[17] In Fairfax County, Virginia, teachers use Monday afternoons for planning. Students are dismissed from school and either go home or to a program organized by the community recreation department.

At the Key School in Indianapolis, Indiana, parents and other community members organize all-school assemblies or special projects for a half day each week so teachers are free to work together.[18] In Southbury, Connecticut, teachers at Gainfield Elementary School organize themselves in teams, with groups rotating their planning sessions every other week. According to principal John Mudry: "If schools don't provide time for their teachers to get together, they merely give lip service to the idea of restructuring."

TABLE 8

HOW OFTEN DO YOU MEET WITH ONE OTHER TEACHER
TO PLAN AND PREPARE TOGETHER?
(PERCENTAGE OF TEACHERS AGREEING)

	SELDOM/ NEVER	SOMETIMES	FREQUENTLY
Russia	63%	34%	3%
Zimbabwe	52	46	2
UNITED STATES	41	42	17
Germany	37	49	14
Chile	36	41	23
China	34	53	13
Turkey	33	46	21
Israel	29	41	30
Mexico	28	50	22
Great Britain	23	50	27
Italy	22	30	48
Japan	16	59	25

SOURCE: The Carnegie Foundation for the Advancement of Teaching and the George
H. Gallup International Institute, The International Schooling Project, 1994.

When the Danebo Elementary School in Eugene, Oregon, began
to reshape its curriculum, teachers discovered, very quickly, they
needed time. With parent and school board approval, the school
day was extended one-half hour, four days a week. With this
extra instructional time, it was possible for classes to end two
hours early on Wednesday. Teachers now meet from noon until
four o'clock every Wednesday afternoon, planning together, sharing ideas. Principal James Winger said: "Teachers now feel like
the professionals they are."[19]

Regardless of the precise arrangement, we cannot stress strongly
enough the importance of giving the principal and teachers time

to plan and work together, and to organize themselves, not just horizontally, but *vertically* as well. Typically, when teacher planning does occur, it is all too often "layered." First-grade teachers meet only with other first-grade teachers, second-grade teachers with second-grade teachers, and on up the line, which leads to a disturbing discontinuity in learning. One first-grade teacher told us: "I have no idea what the third-grade lessons cover."

In the Basic School, teachers from different grade levels work together—with fifth-grade teachers meeting with kindergarten teachers, for example—pursuing common goals and creating a sequential course of study that spirals upward, resulting in a seamless web of learning.

Several years ago, Vegas Verdes Elementary School in Las Vegas, Nevada, organized itself into "teaching families," made up of teachers from kindergarten through grade five. Grade levels became blurred; lesson units were planned for coherence through all the grades. Teachers combined field trips. "Reading buddies" were organized across the grades, with older students tutoring younger ones.[20]

At San Antonio's Jackson-Keller Elementary School, where vertical "family groups" have been formed, third-grade teacher Suzann Westermann said: "Since we've been in families, children and teachers feel a new unity. There's loyalty to one another, too. You get to know children before they come to you, and you watch them grow and progress, moving upward."

TEACHERS AS MENTORS

Basic School teachers, while giving overall direction to the school, are, above all else, *instructional* leaders, who serve both as guides and mentors to their students, encouraging them to become self-directed learners and disciplined, creative thinkers. Educator Theodore Sizer, director of the Coalition of Essential Schools, said it best: "Teachers do not transfer information from the brain of the teacher to the brain of the student, but rather, they make students think. Education is about habits of the mind."[21]

When it comes to *styles of teaching*, effective teachers vary greatly. Some create a structured environment for learning in the classroom; others are more informal. One second-grade teacher said: "I'm not interested in 'telling' children all they need to know. I provide lots of classroom experiences that start them on the path to learning." In contrast, a fourth-grade teacher told us she wanted her lesson plans more structured: "Children like to explore, but they also like to have a product to share with others. I define goals and make assignments."

When we asked elementary school students about the qualities of a good teacher—the characteristics they like most—not surprisingly they rated "understanding student problems" as most important. "Being kind and friendly" also was highly rated by students, along with "setting a good example." "Knowing the subject" was ranked sixth, reflecting the fact, perhaps, that students just assume teachers are well informed (table 9). It seems obvious from these findings that when children walk into classrooms, they are far more concerned about who the teacher *is* than they are about what the teacher *knows*.

In contrast, parents have quite different ideas about the qualities of a good teacher. For example, 86 percent of those we surveyed said that "motivating students to learn" was important, while only 37 percent of the students made this selection. "Being willing to explain things in different ways" also was important to parents. Nearly 40 percent gave "staying in contact with home and parents" high marks—a quality supported by only 9 percent of the students. Only 8 percent of parents viewed "being kind and friendly" as an important quality of a good teacher, a quality students regard highly. Less than a third of the parents chose "understanding student problems" as an important quality. Students, on the other hand, chose this characteristic above all others (table 9).

There is no single path to good pedagogy, no one way of doing things. Students can be inspired in a variety of ways, and we celebrate the rich mosaic of teacher talent we observed in schools from coast to coast. Still, after reviewing the literature, visiting hundreds of classrooms, and talking with teachers and students, we concluded that, in the Basic School, at least four essential characteristics define, in broad terms, the qualities of an effective teacher.

> *First, a good teacher is well informed.* Basic School teachers possess substantial knowledge in the content areas to be taught. They have a solid foundation in liberal studies, with special emphasis on English, mathematics, and the arts. They have, as well, the ability to integrate content across the curriculum, helping students place their learning in a larger context. "A profession can be no better than the knowledge base on which it rests," observes John Goodlad.[22]

TABLE 9

QUALITIES OF A GOOD TEACHER

	PERCENTAGE AGREEING	
	STUDENTS	PARENTS
Understanding student problems	48%	29%
Being kind and friendly	45	8
Setting a good example for the students	39	36
Helping or motivating students to learn	37	86
Willing to explain things in different ways	33	40
Knowing the subject they are teaching	33	33
Helping students memorize facts	18	2
Not playing favorites	14	4
Keeping order in the classroom	12	10
Teaching good habits	9	12
Staying in contact with home and parents	9	38

Source: The Carnegie Foundation for the Advancement of Teaching and the George
H. Gallup International Institute, The International Schooling Project, 1994
(United States); respondents could choose three qualities from a list of eleven.

·   *Second, a good teacher knows children.* Basic School teachers are attentive, always, to the whole child.[23] Trained as observers of children, effective teachers see the vital, inseparable relationship between the intellectual, physical, emotional, social, and moral growth of students. Academic content is crucial. But it is critically important that teachers know about the growth and development of children and are able to relate their knowledge to the readiness of students.

·   *Third, a good teacher empowers students.* Basic School teachers are well grounded in the art of teaching. They use a variety of methods, coaching students, giving guidance. But the successful teacher also encourages students to explore their own questions, moving from the familiar to the unknown. Eleanore Zurbruegg, an award-winning teacher at the Ridgeway Elementary School in Memphis, Tennessee, says: "What a teacher does and says can stay with a child forever. I try to build confidence, awaken curiosity, excite young minds, shape attitudes, encourage discoveries, and invite learning."[24]

· *Fourth, a good teacher is an open, authentic human being.* Basic School teachers are not only educationally and pedagogically well prepared, they also are honest in their relationships with students, and confident. They are willing to be vulnerable and professionally self-revealing, exploring ideas candidly. They convey always to students integrity and warmth. When we think of a great teacher, we remember a person whose qualities are those of a respected and trusted friend.

Much of what we know about good pedagogy includes old-fashioned, yet enduring, qualities that still work—command of the material to be taught, contagious enthusiasm for the work to be done, and optimism about the potential of all children. Good teachers are authentic human beings. Linda Darling-Hammond, a professor at Teachers College, Columbia University, succinctly sums up the teacher's task this way: "Reaching every student rather than covering the curriculum, connecting to all learners rather than merely offering education, is our task."[25]

TEACHERS AS SCHOLARS

Basic School teachers are team members. They serve as mentors to their students. But for these essential roles to be fulfilled, teachers in the Basic School also must be *scholars*, staying well informed and remaining professionally renewed. It seems so obvious: For teachers to inspire students, they themselves must be inspired. After all, continuing education is a requirement for doctors, dentists, lawyers, nurses, architects—why not for teachers, who each day shape the lives of children?

The harsh truth is, however, that staff development is a low priority in most districts. It's true that almost all schools do have two or three "teacher workshop" days each year.[26] But it's also true that all too often these "inservice sessions" are little more than lectures offered by "experts," who are "long on process and short on substance," as one teacher put it, adding that the inservice program at her school is "an example of what a good teacher should *not* do." Sadly, this is not an isolated case. Our international survey revealed that fully 40 percent of the teachers in this country—the highest percentage of all countries surveyed—describe their ongoing training as "disappointing" (table 10).

The vitality of a school is measured, ultimately, by the vitality of each teacher. Thus, staff development is a high priority in the Basic School. Specifically, we recommend that professional renewal seminars be scheduled regularly throughout the year, with teachers themselves being given the responsibility to plan both the content and the presentations.

We further recommend that every Basic School, to enrich its staff development program, establish a formal partnership with a higher

TABLE 10

MOST OF THE TIME I HAVE SPENT IN ONGOING TRAINING
HAS BEEN DISAPPOINTING.

	PERCENTAGE OF TEACHERS RESPONDING "YES"
UNITED STATES	40%
Italy	35
Great Britain	32
Russia	29
Japan	24
Germany	24
Israel	23
Chile	19
China	19
Turkey	14
Mexico	12
Zimbabwe	12

Source: The Carnegie Foundation for the Advancement of Teaching and the George
            H. Gallup International Institute, The International Schooling Project, 1994.

learning institution in the region. A college or university can, without question, be a vital resource to the school, with faculty acting as consultants, and with college students serving as interns at the school, making it possible for teachers to have more planning time.

However, for a school-university alliance to really work, the principal and teachers must be full partners in defining the collaborative agenda. Further, professors who participate in such programs must be rewarded by their university for their work, with the recognition that scholarship involves not only the discovery of knowledge, but its application, too.

The University of Southern California and the Norwood Elementary School in South Central Los Angeles have a collaborative program similar to a "teaching hospital," to borrow a term from medical education. Ten Norwood teachers work as partners with university faculty and students. The university sends staff to the school every day. Norwood teachers, in turn, attend monthly seminars at the university. "Norwood is a setting in which we can provide teachers and student teachers with the tools to create a better school," Hillary Foliart, a university instructor, notes, adding that they, in turn, can help the university improve its work.[27]

Here, then, is our conclusion: In the Basic School, teachers are leaders who work together, stay professionally renewed, and serve as inspired mentors to their students. Cyrilla Hergenhan, an award-winning elementary teacher in Catonsville, Maryland, sums up the teacher's role this way: "I have come this far in my education because I have been lifted up on someone else's shoulders. This is how I see my role as teacher. I lift up my students so they can see into the horizon. I do this knowing that they will have a vision farther than mine."[28]

Parents as Partners

> *In the Basic School, the circle of community extends outward to embrace parents, who are viewed as the child's first and most important teachers. A vital partnership is created between the home and school, one that begins during the preschool years, is strengthened when the child formally enrolls, and continues from kindergarten through grade five.*

"WELCOME" is the first word parents see as they enter the Irving Weber Elementary School in Iowa City, Iowa. This one word vividly captures the spirit of the school. The word is even painted as artwork on wooden ceiling beams spanning the foyer. Down the corridor, just off the media center, parents have a room of their own, a pleasant place with new tables and chairs, books to read, a bulletin board, and coffee. Parents who come into the Irving Weber Elementary School immediately feel at home— "welcome," as the sign says.

Secretary of education Richard Riley recently declared: "The American family is the rock on which a solid education can and must be built."[1] And in the Basic School, the circle of community, which begins with the principal, teachers, and students, quickly extends outward to embrace the family. Parents are, after

all, a child's first and most essential teachers. The greatest milestones in learning occur not in the classroom, but in the home.
This is the place where growth begins, where language is first
encountered, where values first take root.

The home is, without question, the child's first classroom. No
surrogate or substitute arrangement, however well planned or
well intended, can replace a loving, supportive family. Samuel G.
Sava, executive director of the National Association of Elementary School Principals, put it this way: "[C]hildren absorb, by
emotional and intellectual osmosis, as many unspoken lessons
about love and work in their homes as they do the spoken lessons
of the classroom. It's not just speech and early literacy that good
mothers and fathers confer, but flesh-and-blood examples of how
to live."[2]

Research establishes, unequivocally, that parent engagement has
a positive impact on students' academic achievement, behavior
in school, and attitudes about school and work.[3] Further, when
teachers were asked to identify the *one* issue that should receive
the highest priority in public education policy, the vast majority
said "strengthening the parents' roles in their children's education."[4] A recent Gallup poll also revealed that more than 90
percent of parents in this country believe that encouraging greater
parent involvement in their children's education is "very
important."[5]

The problem is, however, that many of today's parents, especially single parents, have so much to do and feel torn between
work and family obligations. Sociologist Arlie Hochschild describes the situation this way: "For all the talk about the impor-

tance of children, the cultural climate has become subtly less hospitable to parents who put children first. This is not because parents love children less, but because a 'job culture' has expanded at the expense of a 'family culture.'"[6]

"I believe parents love their children," said one Connecticut teacher, "but in today's society, everyone works and they are just plain tired." Another teacher in an urban Missouri school said: "Parents really do want to spend more time with their children, but they simply are trying to do too much, without help. It's very hard for them to fit the pieces together."

We hear a lot of talk these days about how schools have failed. But what's becoming clear is that it's not the school that's failed, it's the *partnership* that's failed, with schools taking on responsibilities that families and communities and religious institutions once assumed. Our international survey revealed, for example, that 89 percent of parents in this country believe that "families are not taking enough responsibility for the welfare of their children." This was the highest among all twelve countries in our survey. By way of contrast, only 29 percent of the parents in Israel feel that families are not being adequately responsible for their children (table 11).

Overwhelmingly, parents want to do right by their children. They worry in the dark of night about their future and most parents, even those with busy schedules, would like to be more involved in schools. Frequently, however, they are confused about just how they can most appropriately fit in. And we even heard complaints from some parents that when they did reach out to schools their overtures were rejected. Former secretary of education

TABLE 11

FAMILIES ARE NOT TAKING ENOUGH RESPONSIBILITY
FOR THE WELFARE OF THEIR CHILDREN.

	PERCENTAGE OF PARENTS AGREEING
UNITED STATES	89%
Great Britain	71
Chile	65
Mexico	54
Germany	54
China	53
Zimbabwe	51
Russia	47
Japan	46
Italy	41
Turkey	38
Israel	29

SOURCE: The Carnegie Foundation for the Advancement of Teaching and the George H. Gallup International Institute, The International Schooling Project, 1994.

Terrel Bell summarized the problem this way: "A lot of schools advocate parent involvement, but they don't have a specific program to get it done."[7]

The Basic School has a plan.

PRESCHOOL PARTNERSHIP

Schools cannot and should not replace the family. Still, a close and continuing partnership during the preschool years can improve a child's prospects for school success. "What's needed, many educators believe, is . . . more extensive efforts to provide parents with parenting and educational skills," said Keith Geiger, president of the National Education Association.[8] And in the Basic School, the partnership between home and school begins early to ensure that all children come to school "ready to learn."

Specifically, we recommend that every Basic School establish a Preschool PTA. The aim of such a program is to build a bridge, very early, between the home and school and give helpful guidance to parents who wish to participate. Parenting classes on such topics as language development, how children grow, and playtime and good nutrition could be held at places convenient to parents—in churches, synagogues, Head Start centers, community buildings, housing projects, work sites, and, of course, in the school itself.

Lakewood, Ohio, has a Preschool PTA, an informal network of parents of preschoolers, with three hundred and fifty participating families. Eight neighborhood groups have been organized, and parents get to know their neighbors and receive support. "It is important to know that you are not alone, whether you are a working mom, or a single mom, and that when you have a problem, you have someone to talk to," said Rebecca Sammon, a Lakewood parent. "You borrow ideas from other parents. Some questions may seem silly, like 'How should your child respond to a bully at preschool?' But these are topics important to parents."

A child born in the neighborhood served by the Dann C. Byck Elementary School in Louisville, Kentucky, receives a "Byck Baby" tee-shirt from the school-parent organization. A picture of the newborn is displayed proudly on the school bulletin board, and parents of young children receive child-care brochures. A parent library at the school loans books, toys, and games to the family, and school staff members even help parents negotiate time off from work to attend parenting classes on such topics as how to read and talk with children and how to promote social skills. Before preschool parenting classes began, a majority of the kindergartners at Byck needed remedial help. Today, almost all move on successfully to first grade. "We've discovered that the key to helping the children is involving parents," said Stephanie Hoover, program director.[9]

SCHOOL-ENTRY PARTNERSHIP

One warm September morning, on the first day of school, we visited an elementary school on the outskirts of a large midwestern city. About twenty-eight five-year-olds had congregated outside the door of a kindergarten classroom. Most had walked to school with a parent, guardian, or older sibling. A few had come alone. When the bell rang, the teacher invited the children inside, gave each one a smiling-face nametag, and asked them to form a circle on the floor. After a few reassuring hugs, most parents left. Several entered the classroom, but after standing awkwardly on the edges for several minutes, they too drifted away.

The First Day of School. In the Basic School, the first day of school is a time for bonding, not of separation. Rather than forming a circle on the edges, parents are invited to the center and formally welcomed into the community of learning. Specifically, we recommend that each Basic School have a carefully planned first day of school ceremony, a time when parents and guardians and new students join in celebration, greeted by the principal, teachers, and even, perhaps, school board members. On this celebrative occasion, goals can be discussed, a tour offered, refreshments served. Each new parent and student should be teamed up with a parent and student already enrolled in the school.

We recommend, further, that the first day of school be recognized *nationally* as a day of celebration. For this to be accomplished, we suggest that employers give parents released time to join their children at school. After all, workers are given time off to vote and serve on jury duty. Why not give mothers and fathers time off, with pay, to accompany their child to school? Such a move would say to children that education is indeed a partnership between the home and school.

In Massachusetts, Gov. William F. Weld granted state employees released time "to visit classroom teachers, to volunteer in schools, and to serve in school governance." He also asked other employers to provide time for such activities, beginning at the start of each school year. "I have challenged business to redefine the model of what constitutes good corporate citizenship," he added.[10]

In Cleveland, Ohio, parents, grandparents, and guardians are invited to school for what's called Family Day. To promote participation, over one hundred area employers gave fourteen thousand workers paid time off so parents and others could participate. Family Day is now an annual affair, and the number of participating parents, with employer support, keeps growing. According to Michael Charney, a teacher at Lincoln School in Cleveland, "Family Days are a way to move beyond the hope for parental involvement to signaling, in a concrete way, the parent's place in the school."[11] We're suggesting that the first day of school might be considered "Family Day" in communities all across the nation.

On opening day in Japan, the whole school welcomes first-graders and their families. Children, parents, and grandparents dress in their best clothes, with grandmothers in kimonos. The principal greets the assembly, introduces staff, and talks about school goals. A local town official may speak, lending a community presence. Finally, teachers take students to their rooms, show them their desks, and tell them about procedures. "The total effect of everything is a welcome into a new family," according to author Merry White. "The school is always called 'our' school."[12]

Covenant for Learning. To formalize the home-school partnership, Basic School teachers and parents may wish to enter into a *covenant for learning* at the beginning of the year. By "covenant" we do not mean a formal contract. Rather, we mean a pledge by both partners to participate in the child's learning. Parents might agree, for example, to help the child get to school on time, read to the child, assist with homework, and attend parent-teacher conferences. The school, in turn, might pledge to have clear goals, evaluate carefully the child's progress, and communicate regularly with parents.

Printed as a scroll or certificate, a covenant for learning could be signed as part of the "First Day of School Celebration." Or it could be sent to parents before the start of the school year, and then collected at the ceremonies on opening day. Signing a covenant is, of course, a symbolic act, but if parents and schools would *together* make a cooperative pledge to serve children, the impact would be substantial. Pascal D. Forgione, Delaware's

State School Superintendent, put the challenge this way: "Every school should sit down with parents at the beginning of the school year. Let's get parents involved in understanding the criteria and the quality of work at the very beginning."

St. Ann's School in Somerville, Massachusetts, involves all families in a covenant with the school. Each student and parent, with the teacher, pledges to form a partnership for learning. In Grandview, Missouri, parents pledge, in a learning covenant, to set aside at least twenty minutes each night to help their children with schoolwork. They agree, as well, to attend instructional lessons about the school's reading and math programs.

Reading, Ohio, has a citywide covenant for learning which lists responsibilities not just for parents, but for the *entire* community. "All of this has served to focus on the value of education," says John Varis, Reading's superintendent. "What we have behind us now is the power of everyone in the community thinking about education."[13]

Minneapolis, Minnesota, also introduced a citywide pledge. "The Minneapolis Covenant" includes everyone, from school board members to students. Students pledge to attend school regularly, ask for help, respect other students and adults, and keep the school safe. Parents pledge to help their children attend school on time, keep high expectations, communicate regularly with school staff, and provide a quiet space for homework. School staff, in turn, promise, among other things, to set high expectations, respect cultural differences, and "show that I care about all students."[14]

Student Inventory. At the beginning of the school year, all parents surely must become well informed about the school. It is equally important, however, that the school become knowledgeable about the child.[15] We propose, specifically, a *student inventory* for every Basic School, a simple form that would provide a portrait of each student, with such information as a list of favorite books, toys, and songs, as well as learning milestones, including speech development, and early attempts at drawing and writing.[16]

The child's health history could be recorded, too, with such basics as height, weight, and immunizations, and special medication needs. Once established, the student inventory might be passed along from grade to grade, or follow the child who moves to another school. Confidential information is not what we are talking about. Privacy must be protected. It does seem reasonable, however, for schools to gather basic information about the background and interests of each student, to support learning.

The Forest Park Elementary School in St. Paul, Minnesota, recently began asking parents to list their child's interests and strengths, along with the parents' own goals for their child. The information is then used to develop a Parent-Student-Teacher Plan at the beginning of the school year. The plan is helpful during parent conferences in monitoring how effectively school goals are being met. Such a procedure seems appropriate for every school.

SUSTAINING THE PARTNERSHIP

In the Basic School, the partnership is sustained throughout the year as parents participate in regularly scheduled conferences, as well as informal conversations.[17] Currently, most parents of

TABLE 12

HOW OFTEN DURING THE COURSE OF THE YEAR DO YOU HAVE A
FACE-TO-FACE DISCUSSION ABOUT YOUR CHILD'S WEAKNESSES
AND STRENGTHS WITH YOUR CHILD'S TEACHER?

	PERCENTAGE OF PARENTS AGREEING
More than once a month	5%
About once a month	10
One to three times a year	79
Never	6

SOURCE: The Carnegie Foundation for the Advancement of Teaching and the George H. Gallup International Institute, The International Schooling Project, 1994 (United States).

elementary school children meet with teachers only one to three times a year, according to our survey. Only 10 percent meet as often as once a month (table 12).

Parent Conferences. We recommend at least four formal parent-teacher meetings annually, and ideally, interaction between the home and school is far more frequent.

Centennial Elementary School in Tucson, Arizona, sends home weekly homework packets for students in the early grades, and nightly booklets for students in grades two through five. The school publishes a monthly newsletter with helpful hints for learning and reading at home. Centennial also has an interpreter attend conferences for non-English-speaking parents.[18]

At Westwood Elementary School in Santa Clara, California, a packet of information is sent home to parents every Wednesday, with progress reports, homework assignments, and work samples.

"I look forward to Wednesday as my homework day," said one parent. "I spend two hours going through the three envelopes for my three children, but it is time well spent." Adds another parent: "I very much appreciate the large envelope that comes home each Wednesday. It's an easy way to communicate thoughts and opinions back to teachers." Notes a third parent: "The envelope reminds students that parents know what homework is expected. It makes shirking it a little harder! The weekly communication promotes an all-around unity for child, parent, and the school."[19]

Such intimate interaction between the home and school means adding even more responsibility to a teacher's already overburdened schedule. To provide additional support, Basic Schools may wish to use teacher aides, volunteers from the local university, senior citizens, and even high school students to help out. Teachers simply cannot do it all.

A Parent Place. We also recommend that each Basic School have a parent place, a comfortable location in the building where parents gather throughout the day and mingle, informally, with staff or other parents.[20] In schools where space is tight, chairs might be arranged at the end of a corridor, or near the school office, or a corner in the library might become "the parent place," sending a strong signal to parents that they are considered full members of the school "family."

While visiting an elementary school in the West, we came across a "parent center" that housed, along with a coffee pot and homey furniture, a library of parenting books, tips on how to make a neighborhood walk educational for children, and samples of new children's literature. In another school, we found a "grandparents corner" in the library, with a big rocking chair and a selection of books close by. Every Basic School could create such a place for parents—and grandparents.

Parent Inventory. Every group of parents has substantial talent that can enrich the social and educational program of a school in a variety of ways. Therefore, we recommend that every Basic School conduct an inventory to identify the skills and experience parents have and the kind of volunteer work they might wish to do. Such information could include artistic talent, construction skills, special knowledge acquired from world travels, and interesting hobbies, all of which could enrich the school.

Orchard School in Ridgewood, New Jersey, put together an "Encyclopedia of People" that listed parents' interests. On any given day, mothers and fathers can be seen working in the library, giving classroom talks about their jobs, or serving as art consultants. Orchard School parents have worked with art teacher Tom Wallace to produce a school calendar that features children's drawings. Parents recently spent weekends working side by side with the principal and teachers, raising money to build a new playground and obtaining the necessary permits.

At Dover Elementary School in Westlake, Ohio, parents run a "book publishing center," binding as many as one thousand books a month—books written and illustrated by the students. At Manhattan's Public School 111, parents established English courses for Spanish-speaking parents. And parents at the Fairfax Elementary School in Cleveland built a new play-and-learn facility on the school grounds, with a kindergarten play lot and nature study area.

Again, employers can help promote such participation. State Farm Insurance in Bloomington, Illinois, for example, recently announced it would give its sixty-seven thousand employees paid time off to volunteer in schools.[21] North Carolina National Bank gives employees two hours of paid leave each week to participate in school activities or confer with teachers. The bank also matches, dollar for dollar, an employee's financial contribution to his or her child's school. "Successful parenting is as challenging as successful banking," says one official.[22]

Several years ago, *Hemmings Motor News* began "education participation days." Employees have two days off each year to visit schools, participate in volunteer activities, or observe classes. The program did not evolve from employee pressures; rather, it was initiated by the owners and managers, who made a commitment to family-friendly policies.[23]

The State of California recently passed an initiative called "The Family-School Partnership Act," which allows parents to take off eight hours a month, or up to forty hours each school year, with employer support. "No single factor can impact our children and our schools more positively than parent involvement," said Delaine Eastin, California State Superintendent of Public Instruction.[24]

Parent Coordinators. Finally, each Basic School should, we believe, have a *parent coordinator*, someone specifically designated to lead the home partnership program—greeting parents when they come to school, organizing parent education workshops, helping teachers with voice-mail messages, operating homework hotlines, and arranging home visits. The coordinator could be a parent volunteer, a senior citizen, or a college student fulfilling a commitment to a community service program.

Lowery Elementary School in Houston, Texas, uses a parent coordinator to recruit and work with parent volunteers, with remarkable results. More than six hundred parents now work in twenty-six volunteer programs, logging 13,500 hours of service every year.

Whitcomb Elementary School in Richmond, Virginia, has a paid parent coordinator who schedules "Let's Talk" sessions every Thursday morning. There's a "Coffee with the Principal" meeting once a month.[25] At Public School 199 in Manhattan, the parent coordinator is a teacher who conducts Tuesday evening discussion groups on subjects ranging from "whole language" instruction to home science projects.[26]

Jackson-Keller Elementary School in San Antonio, Texas, is located in a neighborhood with a highly mobile population, surrounded by housing developments and apartments, with many single-parent families. A few years ago, parents were not involved in the school. But the principal, Alicia Thomas, joined by teachers and the children, hosted "Donuts for Dads" and "Muffins for Moms" parties on Saturday mornings in the lobbies of apartments close by. Barriers were broken. Trust was built. Parents became partners. Teachers felt supported. Children were the winners.

The message is clear. It is simply impossible to have an island of excellence in a sea of community indifference, and when parents become school partners, the results can be consequential and enduring.

A CURRICULUM WITH COHERENCE

The Centrality of Language

> *In the Basic School, literacy is the first and most essential goal. All children are expected to become proficient in the written and spoken word. But language in this school is defined broadly to include words, numbers, and the arts—the essential tools of learning which, taken together, help create a curriculum with coherence.*

The Basic School, as a learning community, focuses first on language. Our sophisticated use of symbols, the truly miraculous capacity we have to communicate with each other, sets human beings apart from all other forms of life. "Language is," as MIT professor Steven Pinker reminds us, "so tightly woven into human experience that it is scarcely possible to imagine life without it."[1] No student can educationally and socially succeed without proficiency in the written and spoken word.

Language is, without question, central to all learning. Every student, to be educationally successful, must learn to read with understanding, write with clarity, and speak and listen effectively. In the Basic School, language is defined broadly to include not just words, but also mathematics and the arts—three symbol systems that have their own unique characteristics and, at the same time, relate intimately to each other.

65

At first blush, it may seem odd to refer to mathematics and the arts as languages, and stranger still to suggest that they are connected. But consider for a moment how the pattern of a grandmother's exquisite quilt is both geometric *and* aesthetic. Consider, too, how the rhythmic beat of music also involves measurement, how opera is a blend of song and speech, and how the magnificent double helix, a discovery that broke the genetic code, is not only rational, but beautiful as well.

Great scientists, poets, musicians, and artists understand, almost intuitively it seems, just how closely words and mathematics and the arts relate to one another. Physicist Richard Feynman observed: "You can recognize truth by its beauty and simplicity."[2] And Werner Heisenberg, who pioneered in quantum mechanics, remarked that truth was "immediately found convincing by virtue of its completeness and abstract beauty. Beauty in exact science, no less than in the arts," he says, "is the most important source of illumination and clarity."[3]

When the world-renowned physicist Victor Weisskopf was asked, "What gives you hope in troubled times?" he replied, "Mozart and quantum mechanics."[4] And when Aleksandr Khazanov, a fifteen-year-old winner of the 1995 Westinghouse Science Talent Search, was asked why he stays awake late at night studying mathematics, he replied: "There was never a time in my life when I did not want to do math. It's the way you can apply a lot of connections to make very beautiful ideas, to obtain such beautiful proofs."[5]

Thus, language in the Basic School is defined broadly. Students gain basic proficiency in the language of *words*, in the language of *numbers*, and in the language of the *arts*.[6] While these symbol systems may be taught separately, students also discover that they are connected in compelling ways. Through words, students explore mathematical concepts. Through mathematics, they discover the arts. Through the arts, they also become verbally and mathematically expressive. In the Basic School, language is a curriculum with coherence.

THE LANGUAGE OF WORDS

Language is encountered first before birth, as the unborn infant monitors the mother's voice. With the first breath of life, children become verbally expressive, beginning with cries and coos, then phonemes, followed by isolated words, culminating in two- and three-word sentences that so delight the grownups.[7] Every parent knows the thrill that comes when a young child names an object, recognizes a face—and then gives it a name. In the early years, language quite literally explodes, and by the time a child heads off to school, he or she has, on average, a vocabulary of more than three thousand words.

In the Basic School, students are encouraged to communicate orally, beginning first day of school. They ask questions, listen to poetry, sing together, describe their neighborhood, and are encouraged to play together, which is already going on in many elementary classrooms, according to our research. We found, for example, that, when added together, 37 percent of the nine- to eleven-year-olds we surveyed in this country say their class most often spends time "working in groups" (which they like to do the *most)* and "discussing something together." In contrast, 30 percent of those surveyed report that their class most often spends time "listening to the teacher talk," which is one of the things they like to do the *least* (table 13).

TABLE 13

WHICH ONE OF THESE LEARNING ACTIVITIES IS HAPPENING
MOST OFTEN IN YOUR CLASSES AND
WHICH ONE DO YOU LIKE DOING THE MOST?
(PERCENTAGE OF STUDENTS AGREEING)

	HAPPENING MOST OFTEN	STUDENT PREFERENCE
Listening to the teacher talk	30%	6%
Discussing something together as a class	23	13
Students working on their own	19	14
Working in groups of students	14	47
Answering the teacher's questions	9	9
Listening to a student give a report	3	NA
Repeating aloud together what we need to remember	2	1
Giving an oral report to the class	NA	10

SOURCE: The Carnegie Foundation for the Advancement of Teaching and the George
H. Gallup International Institute, The International Schooling Project, 1994
(United States); NA indicates "not asked."

Teachers surely have an obligation not only to *inform* students, but also to *engage* them. Mortimer Adler, in *The Paideia Proposal*, describes three teaching styles to achieve three goals: *lecturing*, to transmit information; *coaching*, to teach a skill; and *Socratic questioning*, to enlarge understanding. Adler's conclusion, however, is that: "All genuine learning is active, not passive. It involves the use of the mind, not just the memory. It is a process of discovery, in which the student is the main agent, not the teacher."[8]

At an elementary school in the Southwest, the kindergarten teacher invited twenty-three students to join her on the classroom carpet, first day of school. "I'm Mrs. Miller," she said quietly, "and the first thing we're going to do is get to know each other." She then told a brief story about how two bear cubs met along the road, how they introduced themselves, and explained how "we too become acquainted as we speak *and* listen." Several students stood up and proudly announced their names. Others held back. Soon, however, everyone was enthusiastically engaged. The children were then shown a brightly painted stool called The Talking Bench. It could be used, Mrs. Miller said, when "you have something very special to tell the class. And when someone is sitting on The Talking Bench, let's all be very quiet, and *listen* carefully."

Speaking and listening come first. But learning to *read* is, without question, the top priority in elementary education. When we asked teachers about the most important goals at their school, they said, without exception, "Teaching children to read." And the success of every elementary school, ultimately, is judged by the reading proficiency of its students.

What's often forgotten, however, is that reading, just like speech, begins long before school. Even very young children "read" the signs and signals all around them. They become attentive to picture books and the printed page, particularly when encouraged by their parents. Reading expert Bernice E. Cullinan, of New York University, put it well: "Children who sit beside a reader and follow the print from an early age learn to read quite 'naturally.' We know that the 'modeling' has a lasting effect; children do what they see others do."[9] And once children come to school, the teacher's task is to build on the truly remarkable language skills already in place.

Kristy McDaniel, a first-grade teacher in Texas, began the first day of school last fall by asking, "Who in this class knows how to read?" Faces fell, lips pressed shut. Ms. McDaniel switched on the slide projector and, using pictures of local signs, flashed a familiar image on the screen. "Who can 'read' this?" she asked. Recognizing the familiar red, eight-sided sign, a few children answered, "That's '*stop.*'" A green traffic light appeared. "Who can 'read' this?" "That means 'go,'" several children said. "Who knows what this one says?" "McDonald's!" cried the class. The teacher then asked, "Who can read?" Every hand shot up. On this, the first day of school, the mystery of reading faded. The confidence of children soared.

Everyone agrees that all children should learn to read. But how to *teach* reading remains a perennial debate. Some advocate the phonics method. Others stress vocabulary. And today, a widely used approach is one called "whole language."[10] In the Basic School, all three methods are embraced and thoughtfully employed. Learning phonemes, the building blocks of language, surely is important. Developing a rich vocabulary is essential, too. But in the end, reading, in the richest, fullest sense, occurs only as sounds and words are placed in larger context, when language takes on *meaning*.

"Reading for meaning is paramount," according to a report from New Zealand, considered to be the most literate nation in the world. "Reading must always be rewarding. Children learn to read by reading. . . . The best approach to teaching reading is a combination of approaches. The best cure for reading failure is good first teaching." And, the report adds, "The foundations for literacy are laid in the early years."[11] This summarizes, quite nicely, the philosophy of reading in the Basic School.

Children do learn to read in different ways. Therefore, the methods of instruction should fit the child, not the other way around. Further, while Basic School students have special periods of concentrated reading instruction, they also read across the curriculum, with the entire day opened up to language study. And instead of restricting reading to basal textbooks and spelling workbooks, students in the Basic School read poetry and great children's literature such as *The Tale of Peter Rabbit*, *Treasure Island*, or *Robinson Crusoe*. They find stories that truly interest them and also read to classmates stories they, themselves, have written.

Writing is, in fact, the other side of reading. More than any other form of communication, writing demands clarity of expression. It holds students responsible for their words, while also freeing them to engage in a truly creative act. We discovered, however, that for far too many students, writing is a chore.[12]

Writing expert Lucy Calkins, a professor at Teachers College, Columbia University, reminds us that, all too often, reading and writing are brought together in ways that make students want to avoid both. "In our schools, our students tell us they don't want to write," she says. "They need not bother to tell us; we can feel their apathy as they crank out stories that are barely adequate; we can hear their question, 'How long does it have to be?' "[13]

In the Basic School, writing is not copying words. It is not just penmanship, although well-formed letters are valued. Rather, writing is an act of both discipline *and* discovery, one that allows children to be wondrously self-expressive while teaching clear thinking, too. Further, writing in the Basic School is woven through the whole curriculum, from civics to natural science.

Every day, children are expected to write, write, write. One third-grade teacher, who makes writing a part of every lesson, said: "My goal is to have all students leave at the end of the year as good writers, active readers, creative thinkers."

One further point. In the Basic School, verbal literacy means proficiency in *standard American English*. English is, after all, the primary language of our culture,[14] and without such proficiency, a student's prospects for social and economic success are exceedingly diminished. At the same time, Basic School students are encouraged to become familiar with a second language.

We find it distressing that only an estimated 5 percent of America's public elementary schools provide foreign language instruction,[15] and that only 19 percent of elementary school teachers in this country believe that "a great deal of emphasis" should be given to a second language, the lowest among the twelve countries polled. In contrast, more than 70 percent of the teachers in Germany say "a great deal of emphasis" should be given to a second language (table 14).

The question is, of course, *which* language? In some regions of the country, French or German may be most appropriate. In others, Russian or Chinese may be selected. This is something every community should decide. However, if there is no strong local or regional preference, we suggest Spanish.[16]

Spanish is already the most frequently spoken second language in our schools—and our country. By the year 2000, the United States will be home to the world's fifth-largest Hispanic population.[17] Increasingly, our future as a nation is linked to our

TABLE 14

HOW MUCH EMPHASIS OR WEIGHT SHOULD BE GIVEN TO THE
STUDY OF A SECOND LANGUAGE DURING THE YEARS OF
REQUIRED SCHOOLING?

	PERCENTAGE OF TEACHERS RESPONDING "A GREAT DEAL OF EMPHASIS"
Germany	73%
Israel	72
Zimbabwe	67
Turkey	62
Russia	59
Mexico	55
Italy	52
Chile	45
China	42
Japan	26
Great Britain	21
UNITED STATES	19

SOURCE: The Carnegie Foundation for the Advancement of Teaching and the George
H. Gallup International Institute, The International Schooling Project, 1994.

neighbors to the south. Thus, it seems reasonable to suggest that
elementary schools offer Spanish.

Regardless of the language chosen, we urge that foreign language
instruction begin early, certainly by third grade, that it be offered
daily, and be continued through all the grades.[18] We recognize
that there are far too few foreign language teachers available
today and schools may not be able to introduce, at once, a full
foreign language program. However, as a minimum, we urge that
every Basic School introduce, throughout the curriculum, words

and phrases from many languages, teaching students about the wonderfully diverse ways people communicate with each other.

THE LANGUAGE OF NUMBERS

Mathematics is a universal language, the one we use to explore problems of quantity, space, and time and to be aesthetically expressive, too. University of Chicago mathematician Zalman Usiskin puts it this way: "Previously, math was taught as almost a code—one that only the very bright or math-oriented students could decipher. Math is," he added, "a language, in every sense of the word. It is a way of describing, relating to, and solving the problems of everyday life."[19]

In the Basic School, students learn the fundamentals of mathematics—adding, subtracting, multiplying, and dividing. They learn to compute, measure, estimate, collect and organize data, and explore geometric patterns. Students then move on to higher order skills, such as analysis and problem-solving, discovering that mathematics can be used to understand their world.

Just as with words, children learn the language of mathematics very early. They show great curiosity about round pegs and square blocks long before school. Young children are fascinated by different shapes and sizes and by how things fit together—or don't fit. Preschoolers begin to count things. They notice the symmetry of bridges, the shapes of buildings, and sing songs about ten fingers and ten toes.[20]

The California Mathematics Curriculum Guide vividly describes how math enriches a child's world: "It is natural for children to seek order and beauty and consistency. From the very beginning of a child's life, he or she is searching to organize and understand his or her world. Children notice size and shape and position. They wonder how long, how big, how much. Mathematical thinking is that which helps us to make connections, to see order and logic. It is seeing patterns and making predictions."[21]

For many children, this curiosity about mathematics quickly tapers off.[22] From what we observed in classrooms, it is easy to see why. We found young students spending lots of time filling in worksheets, soaking up numbers, with little understanding of either the problems or the underlying process. Good students get stimulating instruction, while "slow learners" often are engaged in endless drill. Further, lessons frequently are not linked to children's lives. Shirley Frye, former president of the National Council of Teachers of Mathematics, put the problem this way: "Too often, when students ask why they'll need math, we answer that they'll need it for the next lesson or the next course."[23]

Mathematics, when well taught, is very much a part of life.[24] We saw the beauty of mathematics in Kristin Sonquist's classroom at the Downtown Open School in Minneapolis, where origami is taught both as art and geometry. At the Santa Rita School in Los Altos, California, students have used mathematics to estimate the resources used (and wasted) at the school. They draw maps to scale, regularly weigh and measure objects, and chart results. During science experiments, students draw graphs, and in physical education, they measure the distances in races, using addition, subtraction, multiplication, and division. In art, they study geometric designs. In this school, the language of numbers is everywhere.[25]

At Goodwood Elementary School in Baton Rouge, Louisiana, students work with Lego Logo building blocks and a computer to master math concepts. They use bottle caps, straws, toothpicks, "anything to give our students a hands-on experience with mathematics," says Brenda Sterling, principal. First-graders learn graphing and estimation by charting the weather each month. Looking at a graph, children compare the numbers of sunny and overcast days, learning about *less* and *more*. Students track birthdays and lost teeth, learning about probability and statistics.[26]

In the Basic School, children discover mathematics as a language of both order and beauty, one that is woven throughout the curriculum, touching every subject. "For elementary graduates, knowing and doing in mathematics should be inseparable from each other," declares the Council for Basic Education.[27] And one might add, *enjoying*, too.

THE LANGUAGE OF ART

Art, too, is a universal language—perhaps the most evocative form of human expression. Through singing and painting and dancing, it is possible for people of different backgrounds to communicate powerfully their feelings and ideas. The arts give rise to many voices, and make it possible for people who are socially, economically, and ethnically separated to understand one another at a deeper, more authentic level. The arts help build community.

For the most intimate and most deeply moving experiences, people of all ages have, throughout the years, turned to art.

"Artists speak to us in a language that carries meaning that cannot be conveyed through words," says Elliot W. Eisner, Stanford University professor.[28]

The arts are especially appealing to children. A sense of imagery is with us from birth, and youngsters, responding to this deep urge, paint with their fingers, dance to the beat of drums, sing simple melodies, make sculptures from modeling clay. For young children, art is *not* a frill; it is an essential language that makes it possible to communicate feelings and ideas words cannot express.

Harvard University psychologist Howard Gardner, in his significant work *Frames of Mind*, reminds us that a child's potential includes what he calls visual and musical intelligence.[29] Jane Alexander, chairman of the National Endowment for the Arts, states that: "Art is a great tool for developing our intellectual, emotional, and aesthetic tastes and capacities."[30]

Further, there is growing evidence that the various dimensions of intelligence—from the verbal to the aesthetic—reinforce each other. Research at New York University, for example, revealed that critical thinking skills in the arts are transferred to other subjects,[31] which is something Ann Alejandro, a teacher in the Rio Grande Valley in South Texas, observes in her classroom everyday: "I am convinced of the parallels between teaching children how to draw and teaching them how to read and write. In all cases, students need to learn *how to see*, to interpret data from the word, the canvas, and the page."[32]

We find it deeply distressing that, in spite of the power and importance of art, many schools consider it to be an "extra," the last subject to come and the first to go. Further, many teachers do not feel comfortable teaching art. And while most elementary teachers believe that language arts and mathematics should receive "a great deal of emphasis," only 25 percent say that the arts should be emphasized in school, according to our survey (table 15).

Weaving the arts through the whole Basic School curriculum, and giving more focused time to art instruction, as well, profoundly enriches students' lives and stimulates their minds. In the Basic School, instructional time is set aside for art, just as for English and math. The children learn artistic skills, as well as being free to "color outside the lines." They draw and paint, sculpt with clay, and build architectural structures.

Each Basic School student also has a musical instrument, beyond the human voice, and plays melodies each day. We suggest a recorder, a simple, inexpensive, yet beautiful instrument which every child, and every teacher, can learn to play. In the upper grades, students may wish to select their own special instrument— a flute, a trumpet, violin, or drums.

Children in the Basic School also experience art through dance. Jacques D'Amboise, the internationally renowned dancer and founder of the National Dance Institute, notes that dance is a language all its own, one that builds confidence and intelligence in children. Much of dance embraces the language of mathematics, for example, as students study choreographic patterns. "Dance is the most immediate and accessible of the arts because it involves your own body," he says. D'Amboise concludes that by learning to be expressive through dance, young students are, quite literally, taking control of their own lives.[33]

TABLE 15

"A GREAT DEAL OF EMPHASIS" SHOULD BE GIVEN TO
EACH OF THE FOLLOWING SUBJECTS:
BASIC LANGUAGE SKILLS, MATHEMATICS, AND THE ARTS
(PERCENTAGE OF TEACHERS AGREEING)

	BASIC LANGUAGE SKILLS	MATHEMATICS	THE ARTS
Great Britain	98%	91%	17%
Zimbabwe	98	90	63
Germany	94	50	22
Russia	94	67	51
Chile	94	76	66
UNITED STATES	90	93	25
Japan	90	47	24
Israel	90	85	42
Turkey	89	75	48
China	82	81	12
Mexico	79	89	49
Italy	52	66	24

SOURCE: The Carnegie Foundation for the Advancement of Teaching and the George H. Gallup International Institute, The International Schooling Project, 1994.

In the Basic School, art is an integral language, with a role to play in teaching all the disciplines. And teachers who themselves are not skilled artists include art experiences in their lessons.

At Brumfield Elementary School in rural Princeton, Indiana, art is woven into all aspects of school life. It's integrated into thematic lesson plans on animals, history, and the traditions in other countries. Students design sets for school plays and musicals. Every child has art work displayed. Local residents offer workshops on weaving, painting, wood carving, and folk music.

Students receive instruction in recorders, autoharp, rhythm instruments, as well as vocal music. Artists-in-residence offer workshops on story-building and writing folktales. Recent visitors included a jazz guitarist, a synthesizer specialist, a puppet production company, a square-dance group, and a folk group. At Brumfield, art is an essential language.[34]

The first goal of the Basic School is literacy for all. The aim is for all children to be successful, not just in reading, writing, and mathematics, but also in the universal language we call art. In the end, language study in the Basic School is not just another subject. Rather, it is the most essential tool for learning, the means by which students become both educationally and socially empowered. Lewis Thomas captured the essence of the Basic School when he wrote, childhood is for language.[35]

The Core Commonalities

In the Basic School, all students become well informed. They study the various fields of knowledge,
which are organized, thematically, within a framework called the "Core Commonalities." These eight
commonalities, based on shared human experiences,
integrate the traditional subjects, helping students
see connections across the disciplines and relate
what they learn to life.

While visiting a large elementary school in an eastern city, we
met with a group of gifted teachers during lunch break to talk
about the curriculum at their school. We asked, "Is there general
agreement about what all students should learn?" After a brief
exchange, everyone agreed, without dissent, that each teacher
works alone, and that there is no consensus about what the
curriculum should include. One teacher told us: "The curriculum
at our school seems forever blurred. Everyone has a separate
priority and even though the state has mandates, they're very
broad and no clear pattern has emerged."

Once, there seemed to be general agreement about what information and understanding should be passed on from one generation

to the next. Schools felt quite confident about the content to be covered. Today, no such confidence exists. Everyone agrees that children should learn to read, write, and compute—and the majority of instructional time in the elementary school is devoted to "the basics." But beyond English and arithmetic, and perhaps some science and social studies, we found little agreement about what all elementary school children should know and be able to do.

Children come to school to learn. There *is* content to be studied in the traditional disciplines of science, history, civics, literature, and the rest. And, in the Basic School, students are expected to be well informed about the world, to become "culturally literate," to use E. D. Hirsch's helpful formulation.[1] Albert Shanker reminds us that: "Children are not born with disciplinary knowledge. . . . If the schools are failing our students . . . [i]t is because we are satisfied with the shallow kind of knowledge that comes from insufficient grounding in the basic disciplines."[2]

But becoming knowledgeable in the separate academic subjects, while important, is not sufficient. To be truly educated, a student must also make connections across the disciplines, discover ways to integrate the separate subjects, and ultimately relate what they learn to life. British philosopher Lionel Elvin reminds us: "When you are out walking nature does not confront you for three-quarters of an hour only with flowers and in the next only with animals."[3] All parts of the natural world are blended in a majestic, inspiring way. So is a good curriculum.

Little children, when they come to school, keep asking *why*, searching for the hidden threads that link all subjects. But then somewhere around grade four they stop asking *why* and begin to ask, "Will we have this on the test?" "What happens," Mortimer Adler asks, "between the nursery and college to turn the flow of questions off?"[4] What happens is a focus on fragments of information, rather than authentic, integrative questions. Students study the separate subjects. They pick up isolated facts, but what they fail to gain is a coherent view of knowledge and a more integrated, more authentic, view of life.

An educational approach that lacks unity will not touch the child's deepest self nor stir within each student a heightened appreciation of the mystery and majesty of the world. Further, studies on the workings of the human mind reveal that learning, at its best, is an *integrative* function. In a comprehensive review of neuroscience research, Renate and Geoffrey Caine concluded that in learning, the brain is constantly synthesizing things, organizing knowledge, and processing parts of information into a whole.[5]

The irony is that neither students *nor* teachers seem satisfied with the piecemeal approach to learning that seems to fragment the curriculum today. For example, when we asked teachers across the country if they thought the curriculum is best taught as "separate" or as "integrated" subjects, nine out of ten supported the integrated approach (table 16). One teacher said: "I'm not interested in presenting isolated facts which children seem to memorize and forget. I want to help students put each lesson in perspective."

Creative teachers, dissatisfied with fragments, often design their own integrated units on such themes as space travel, the rain

TABLE 16

WHICH IS CLOSER TO YOUR VIEW OF HOW TO
PRESENT THE CURRICULUM MOST EFFECTIVELY?

	PERCENTAGE OF TEACHERS AGREEING
Integrate subjects	89%
Teach each subject separately	11

SOURCE: The Carnegie Foundation for the Advancement of Teaching and the George H. Gallup International Institute, The International Schooling Project, 1994 (United States).

forest, immigrants, and the like. This is surely helpful. The problem is that, while connections may occur *within* each of these units, somehow the separate lesson plans never seem to fit together. Here's what one third-grade teacher said: "I feel really good about the integrated units in social studies I've put together for the year. But, frankly, I still don't see how they relate to an overall plan. Each unit simply stands alone."

Clearly, what is urgently needed, in every elementary school, is *a curriculum with coherence*, one that moves beyond the separate subjects, helps students see relationships and patterns and apply learning thoughtfully to their own lives. But how is this to be accomplished? Is it possible to organize what we teach in school in a way that is both comprehensive *and* coherent?

What we propose, in the Basic School, is not so much a new *curriculum* as a new way to *think* about the curriculum. Again, there *is* a core content to be learned in history, literature, science, civics, and the other fields of academic study. However, in the Basic School, this traditional content is fitted within eight integrative themes we have named the "Core Commonalities."[6] Students begin exploring these commonalities in kindergarten, and continue to learn about them in a curriculum that spirals upward, with increasing complexity, from one grade level to the next.

By "core commonalities" we mean those universal experiences that are shared by all people, the essential conditions of human existence that give meaning to our lives. These include: *The Life Cycle, The Use of Symbols, Membership in Groups, A Sense of Time and Space, Response to the Aesthetic, Connections to Nature, Producing and Consuming,* and *Living with Purpose.* Within these eight themes, every traditional subject or academic discipline can, we believe, find a home.

The eight core commonalities listed above are presented in an order that seems to reflect how they actually evolve in life itself, starting with birth, and followed by language. Young children then discover that they are a member of groups, beginning with the family. They soon develop a conscious awareness of themselves in time and space. Children respond to the aesthetic, and, over time, realize they are connected to the natural world, learning such things as where their food comes from. As they mature even more, they learn how to make and use things. Later, children are asking the consequential questions about the meaning and purposes in life.

By focusing on these common *human* experiences, children not only acquire a core of knowledge, they also discover relationships across the separate subjects. They begin to see how what they study in the classroom actually relates to *them*, how their own lives can develop in a personally, socially, and ethically constructive way. Students learn, as well, that the human experiences we all share are lived out in very different ways from one culture to another.

What follows, then, is a brief sketch of the integrated curriculum of the Basic School and what each of the eight commonalities might include.

THE LIFE CYCLE

The Goal: All Basic School students understand that human life has a beginning, a time of growth, and an ending. They acquire a basic knowledge of the body's needs and its functions, and adopt personal habits that promote wellness. They develop an appreciation for the sacredness of life, and understand how life experiences differ from one culture to another.

All people share the sacredness of life. And at the very core of the Basic School curriculum is a study of *The Life Cycle*. This commonality, which draws upon such traditional subjects as health, nutrition, hygiene, and physical education, enables students to learn about the human body, growth and development, good health habits, and, above all, gain respect for the miracle of life.

Children are endlessly curious about life. They are always asking questions: "Why can't babies talk?" "What's inside an egg?" "Why is my mother sick?" "Why do plants need water?" "How do I grow?" "Why do people die?" This curiosity, this steady flow of questions, should be responded to sensitively, respecting the readiness level of the child. Yet, all too often, important questions about life go unanswered, and students leave school often knowing more about their Walkmans and VCRs than they do about the miracles of their own bodies.

In his book *Joys and Sorrows*, cellist Pablo Casals speaks eloquently about what we should teach our children when they inquire about life. "We should say to each of them: Do you know what you are? You are a marvel. You are unique. In all of the world there is no other child exactly like you. In the millions of years that have passed there has never been another child like you. And look at your body—what a wonder it is! your legs, your arms, your cunning fingers, the way you move! . . . Yes, you are a marvel. And when you grow up, can you then harm another who is, like you, a marvel? You must cherish one another."[7]

Young children begin the study of the human life cycle by observing other forms of life, gerbils perhaps or baby chicks. They consider how animal young enter the world, learn about eggs set afloat in the ocean, and examine nests warmed by a mother bird. They watch trees change through the seasons, and write stories about pets. Later, students begin to study their own bodies, learn the benefits of exercise, and begin to understand how our bodies are nourished. They learn, too, about the damage done by tobacco, alcohol, and certain drugs.

Basic School students, while studying The Life Cycle, also make connections across the generations. Mothers with infants or toddlers visit school so young children can observe, firsthand, the wondrous changes that occur in the early stages of life. Students visit retirement villages, too, inviting senior citizens, sometimes grandparents, to serve as mentors, learning lessons that span the generations.

The Life Cycle, like the other commonalities, spirals upward, from kindergarten to grade five—moving from the simple to the more complex. And at the completion of this study, students will have discovered that the cycle of life is, indeed, something we all share. They will have learned, at a basic level, how the body functions and how to stay healthy. They will see the cycle of life around them, in nature, how it differs in other cultures, and, above all, begin to appreciate the sacredness of their own lives and the lives of others.

THE USE OF SYMBOLS

The Goal: All Basic School students understand that people communicate with each other through symbol systems. They explore the history of language, consider the purposes of communication, learn about new technology, and discover how mass communication can enhance or diminish human understanding. And they discover that integrity is the key to authentic human interaction.

After life, comes language. We all communicate with one another. And this second commonality, *The Use of Symbols*, introduces students to the miracle of words, not just as a basic skill, but as a "system of symbols." Most elementary students are often taught only the *techniques* of language. They study language as a tool, learning grammar, parts of speech, how to spell, and how to write a sentence or a paragraph. Rarely are they asked to step back and reflect upon the process itself, to consider language as a social function, and how it connects people to each other. This is so important, yet it's hardly ever taught.

In this commonality, children begin to put language in social, historical, and ethical perspective. They explore, through all six grades, such questions as: "How did I learn to speak?" "When did writing begin?" "What symbols did people use long ago?" "How many languages are there?" "How do I know if someone is telling the truth?" "Do languages change?" "Is what I see on TV real?"

The Use of Symbols introduces students to the history of language. They learn how people first made paper long ago, sent messages, used drumbeats or smoke signals, and drew pictures on the walls of caves. They begin to think about how other forms of life—birds, dolphins, bumblebees—send signals to each other. Students also consider the many ways they, themselves, communicate using words, or facial expressions, or body language. And they study the signs and symbols in their own neighborhoods.

Older students learn that we communicate for different reasons: to *inform*, to *persuade*, to *entertain*, and to *inspire*. They consider how words can hurt, as well as heal. Students begin to see how rich and varied language is, and how languages vary from one region or culture to another. They learn, too, about dialects and discover colloquial expressions, and examine, as well, the variety of languages spoken by the ancestors of students in their own classroom.

Before leaving the Basic School, students are introduced to mass communication. They consider how television, movies, and musical recordings influence their own lives, and they begin to make discriminating judgments. By the end of their study, Basic School students not only learn to *use* words, they learn to *think* about them. They are introduced to the *history* of language, the *social significance* of language, and the *ethics* of language. Above all, students learn that language is a sacred trust, and that honesty is the obligation we assume when we are empowered with words.

MEMBERSHIP IN GROUPS

The Goal: All Basic School students understand that everyone holds membership in a variety of groups, beginning with the family. They consider how organizations shape our lives, how we, in turn, can shape institutions, and they develop, in the end, a sense of civic and social responsibility.

We all hold membership in groups. It's an experience we all share. Everyone, from the first to the last moment of their lives, is shaped by social institutions and will, in turn, help shape them. Nearly one hundred and fifty years ago, Ralph Waldo Emerson observed: "[W]e do not make a world of our own, but fall into institutions already made and have to accommodate ourselves to them."[8]

In the study of this commonality, *Membership in Groups*, students might consider: "Which groups did I join at birth?" "Which groups do I belong to?" "Why do people join groups?" "Can I leave a group?" "Why are groups important?" "Does the group make me do things I don't want to do?" "How do groups help my life?" "What does it mean to be a citizen?"

Membership in Groups focuses first on the *family*, described by historian Will Durant as the nucleus of civilization.[9] Students discover the importance of the family unit in society and in their own lives. They consider, too, the informal groups of which they are a part—the clubs, even cliques, that are organized in neighborhoods and on playgrounds. Students also begin to think about the significant role of community groups, service clubs, and religious institutions. They ask: "Why do people come together in these ways?" "How do groups help our community?" They also study the school itself, the institution in which they all hold membership, and ask: "How does it work?" "How many groups are there within our school?"

At the start of each school year, Basic School students may list the groups they belong to, and discuss them throughout the year. They might keep an inventory of their social relationships as they move along and consider, too, the ways various groups affect them. Older students might focus specifically on one group in their own neighborhood. How did it begin? Who's in charge? What's its purpose?

This commonality, like all the others, spirals upward, beginning with simple concepts about groups and membership, and ending with a more deeply rooted understanding of how and why people come together. For example, students in the upper grades begin the study of *civics*. They learn how government functions in their own community and at the national level, and are introduced to such essential documents as the Declaration of Independence, the Constitution, and the Bill of Rights.

By the end of their study, students see themselves as holding membership in a variety of groups, beginning with the family.

They understand how groups are formed, learn about groups locally and nationally, and gain respect for democratic traditions. They are challenged to be a good citizen in their school and beyond, understanding that group membership means having responsibilities, as well as rights.

A SENSE OF TIME AND SPACE

The Goal: *All Basic School students learn that people every-where have the miraculous capacity to place themselves in time and space. Students explore our shared sense of time through history and through intergenerational connections. They learn about our nation's history and study the traditions of other cultures. And they gain perspective, as well, about where they are located, spatially, on the planet and in the universe.*

As a condition of being human, everyone has the truly awesome capacity to recall the past, anticipate the future, and orient them-selves in space. In the study of this commonality—*A Sense of Time and Space*—children begin to put the human experience, and their own lives, in perspective.

With *A Sense of Time*, we all are able to look in both directions— recalling the past and anticipating the future. As T. S. Eliot wrote: "Time present and time past / Are both perhaps present in time future, / And time future contained in time past."[10]

Through a study of history, in particular, with an introduction to archeology, students seek answers to a host of questions: "How many grandparents and great-grandparents do I have?" "What country did my family come from?" "When did they leave?" "How did America begin?" "How far back does time go?" "How can we really know what happened in the past?" "When did the dinosaurs live?" "Will I ride in a spaceship sometime?" "What will life be like for my grandchildren?"

Young children begin their journey through time by thinking about their own histories, creating a family tree perhaps. They imagine what it would be like to live in the time of their grand-parents. They recreate the past—bake bread, make candles, dress in period costumes. Young students also talk with older people about what life was like "long ago," and celebrate the rich heritage of family traditions in their own classroom. They learn about how their school got started and when the community where they live was settled.

Older students study the history of their home state and region, as well as the history of the United States. They research regional folklore and the cultural contributions of various groups in their area. They read biographies of native peoples, of explorers, of pioneers, and learn about leaders both locally and nationally who shaped our nation. A Sense of Time also extends into the future, and students are asked to think about what life may be like for their grandchildren. They create time capsules and consider how decisions made today will surely shape the future—for themselves and for their children.

In *A Sense of Space*, students orient themselves physically to their surroundings. They gain perspective about where they fit through a study of geography and astronomy. Once again, this commonality responds to children's questions: "How deep is the ocean?" "How far is it to the nearest star?" "How does the sun know to come up?" "Where do rivers begin?" "Why are mountains so high?" "What is a comet?"

In this commonality, children study maps and use globes. They identify local landmarks, locate themselves in their own neighborhood, learn about the earth's oceans, major mountain ranges, continents, great rivers, and deserts. Students also study stars and the planets, and—with telescopes and computers—travel to galaxies beyond. Older students examine the solar system, study flight and space travel, turning classrooms into "space stations."

At the completion of this study, students have a basic core of knowledge about the history of the United States and the region where they live. They know something about geography and astronomy. They understand how we all recall the past, anticipate the future, and place ourselves in space. Above all, students begin to feel a part of the continuum of time, and marvel at the majesty of the universe of which they are a part.

RESPONSE TO THE AESTHETIC

The Goal: All Basic School students understand that people respond to beauty and can be expressive in the arts. They explore the rich variety of artistic expression, learning about the various works of art, recognizing the benefits of making art, and knowing some of the ways in which visual and performing arts have evolved in different cultures.

There is something deep within the human spirit that is stirred by beauty. It's a universal experience we all share. Conductor Murray

Sidlin put it this way: "When words are no longer adequate, when our passion is greater than we are able to express in a usual manner, people turn to art. Some people go to the canvas and paint; some stand up and dance. But we all go beyond our normal means of communicating and *this* is the common human experience for all people on this planet."[11]

This commonality, *Response to the Aesthetic*, goes beyond art as a basic tool and introduces students to the formal study of art. It responds to such questions as: "Why do musical instruments make different sounds?" "What's a poem?" "Why does the artist paint that way?" "Is it all right to color outside the lines?" Students discover that art is a profoundly significant human experience woven through history and across cultures. They begin to understand how art shapes our lives.

Basic School students begin their study of this commonality by looking at the beauty all around them—the shape of buildings, the setting of the sun. They watch artists work and talk about their own art. Students look at famous paintings, comparing form and color. They learn to *make* music and also learn *about* music.[12]

Listening to a performance by the high school orchestra, Basic School students may be taken on a "symphony safari," walking through the various sections of the orchestra, listening to the violins, touching the flutes and drums, learning the names of instruments, and what "percussion" means. Students listen to folk music and consider how musical instruments differ from culture to culture.

Students also are introduced, at a basic level, to the world of dance, its history, and the various dance forms. They put on plays and learn to place drama in larger context. In a play about Helen Keller, for example, students might talk about deafness, how the play portrays what it is like to be blind, and how it dramatizes growing up in the South in the late 1800s.

In summary, Response to the Aesthetic introduces young students to a formal study of the arts. Children, through this commonality, begin to understand and respond to aesthetics—to music, dance, theater, and the visual arts—and see how they are woven through history. Above all, students begin to understand that "beauty," in all its forms, enables people to be truly self-expressive, a quality that is not just desirable, but essential, if we are to survive with civility and with joy.

CONNECTIONS TO NATURE

The Goal: All Basic School students recognize that everyone is connected to the natural world. They learn about the scientific method and, in the process, increase their understanding of the world around them. Above all, students discover the beauty and wonder of nature and develop a profound respect for it.

We are all connected to the natural world. Scientist and essayist Lewis Thomas said: "There are no solitary, free-living creatures: Every form of life is dependent on other forms." And this commonality, *Connections to Nature*, responds to questions such as: "Why is the sky blue?" "Where do rivers go?" "Why does a plant grow up?" "What is a rainbow?" "Where do birds go in the winter?" "Why does it rain?" "Why is the sun hot?" "What does 'science' mean?"

In the study of this commonality—which draws upon such subjects as biology, botany, zoology, and geology—students learn about the physical world around them. They begin to understand how plants, animals, and humans relate to the natural environment and how, through science, we learn how nature works.

Children are natural observers, and in the Basic School they look carefully at trees, shrubs, water, and rocks. They study a flock of pigeons finding shelter in the half-hidden gargoyles of the stone church across the street. They watch the family of sparrows weaving a nest in the concavity of the alarm bell at the firehouse next door. They observe carefully as an army of ants marches across the city sidewalk, and learn about nature's division of labor and the recycling of waste.

Basic School students, while visiting the city park or hiking on a trail, select rocks of special interest, identify trees, or study insects and wildflowers. And every classroom in the school includes a garden space so children can study closely, over time, the growth of plants. These observations give children invaluable insight about growth, adaptability, and survival. "All understanding begins with wonder," said the poet and scientist Goethe.[13]

Older students learn about scientists and inventors. They write about the lives of great scientists and discuss the issues they hear in the news—acid rain, the tropical rain forest, the Clean Air Act. Students begin, themselves, to use the scientific method, perhaps by setting up a weather station to track climate changes or by conducting experiments that test the growing rates of fungi or plant life.

After completing this commonality, Basic School students will have acquired a basic knowledge about the natural world. They will know, at a beginning level, the steps of scientific discovery, and will have begun to understand how we are all connected to the natural world. Above all, students will have begun to develop a reverence for the beauty and wonder of the world.

PRODUCING AND CONSUMING

The Goal: All students learn that people, as a part of being human, engage in making and using things. They recognize the value and dignity of work, distinguish wants from needs, and understand the importance of becoming creative producers, informed consumers, and responsible conservers.

Work is universal. All human beings, sometime in their lives, participate in producing and consuming. It's something we all do. In this commonality, *Producing and Consuming*, students begin to learn about the basics of economics, various kinds of careers, how products are made, and the importance of not wasting things. They begin by asking: "Where do grownups go off to every morning?" "How is a car made?" "Where does money come from?" "How does food get to the store?" "How do people start a business?"

In the study of Producing and Consuming, children learn, first, how to make things. Every child becomes familiar with at least one handicraft. They knit a scarf, make wooden bookends, or care for a garden, learning the difficulty and the satisfaction of actually producing something from beginning to end. Young students learn about work from adults who visit the school, and they may also visit the work places of their parents, or other places of work in their own neighborhoods—traveling to art supply houses, paint shops, banks, and supermarkets.

Older students learn about how work has changed throughout the years, why most people today live in cities, rather than on farms. They consider why the self-sufficient agricultural community, idealized in such works as Laura Ingalls Wilder's *Little House* books, no longer characterizes life for most of us today.

Students in the Basic School learn about U.S. currency and, at a basic level, about the exchange of goods and services. Students may create a business—run a "bank" in their classroom, open a school bookstore, or design a recycling plan for their school. In career studies, older students also research a single career—electrical engineering, postal work, architecture, plumbing, the practice of law, or computer programming—sharing what they learn with the class.

By the end of the Basic School, students begin to learn that life, for all of us, involves producing and consuming. They discover the importance and dignity of work, begin to distinguish wants from needs, and understand the importance of carefully using the precious resources of our earth, becoming responsible producers, consumers, and conservers.

LIVING WITH PURPOSE

The Goal: All Basic School students learn that all people seek meaning and purpose for their lives. They understand the importance of values and ethics, learn how religious experience has consequentially shaped the human experience, and begin to see the significance of service.

Everyone seeks fulfillment. We all want meaning in our lives. And the eighth commonality, *Living with Purpose*, brings together topics from many subjects—ethics, philosophy, sociology, and religion for young students. It includes a study of heroes in history, lessons on the value of vocation, and the significance of service. Reinhold Niebuhr observed that man cannot be whole unless he is committed, because he cannot find himself without finding a purpose beyond himself.[14]

This commonality responds to questions such as these: "What makes people happy?" "What's wrong with being mean?" "Are big league ballplayers really heroes?" "Why should I help somebody?" "How many religions are there?" "Are some people better than others?"

Today, many children grow up without a deeply rooted sense of purpose. They feel unneeded, disconnected from the larger world, with few heroes. Many do not feel challenged or inspired. In this study, Living with Purpose, Basic School children are asked to think about people they admire, write about them, and tell why they respect them. They choose heroes in history, as well as those in their own neighborhood who might visit the classroom to talk about their goals and about what has brought meaning to their life. Students, while reading classical literature, discuss how great scientists, artists, and religious leaders lived their daily lives with purpose. They consider, too, how various vocations enrich life, leading to fulfillment, discussing what Benjamin Franklin meant when he wrote in *Poor Richard's Almanac*: "The noblest question in the world is 'What good may I do in it?' "[15]

While public schools are constitutionally restricted from religious practice and instruction, they can teach *about* religion, addressing the powerfully influential role religion has played in all aspects of human history. Consider, for example, that students cannot know the history and meaning of art without encountering religious inspiration—from the Hindu cave paintings and the Buddhist art of Asia, to the Western art tradition.

Students cannot know literature without understanding how religion has shaped the world's great writers, from the historians and playwrights of ancient Greece to writers and poets of our own day. Students cannot learn and understand great music without understanding its influence on performers and composers. Students cannot understand the heritage of the United States, or the history of other countries, without knowing that religion has been a central thread in the fabric of all history.

Finally, Basic School students are encouraged to participate in service. Martin Luther King, Jr., said, "Everybody can be great, because everybody can serve."[16] And beginning with simple chores at home, at school, and in the neighborhood, students can learn that life takes on meaning as we reach out to others. Prof. William Damon of Brown University puts the challenge this way: "Without learning an obligation to serve and respect others, children cannot develop a sense of social responsibility. . . . [T]his is the gravest danger in societies that have lost touch with the need to foster in their children an obligation to serve others."[17]

By the time they move on to middle school, Basic School students will have learned that living with purpose is a universal urge, something we all share. They discover that having honorable goals, diligently pursued, and reaching out to others can assure a life of purpose.

In summary, what we've presented in this chapter is a new way to organize the curriculum in the elementary school. Through a study of eight core commonalities, students become knowledgeable in all subjects now being taught. But it would be a big mistake to view the Core Commonalities curriculum as simply a convenient way to repackage the disciplines, giving the old structure new labels. Rather, beyond becoming well informed, students also discover how the separate subjects are connected and, above all, understand, at a very basic level, these fundamental truths:

· we all share the sacredness of life,
· we all send messages to each other,
· we all belong to groups and institutions,
· we all place ourselves in time and space,
· we all respond to the aesthetic,
· we're all inseparably a part of nature,
· we're all engaged in producing and consuming,
· and we all seek to live with purpose.

Simply stated, the curriculum of the Basic School helps students make connections, integrate knowledge, and relate the lessons of the classroom to their own lives. More than fifty years ago, Mark Van Doren wrote: "The connectedness of things is what the educator contemplates to the limit of his capacity. . . . The student who can begin early in his life to think of things as connected . . . has begun the life of learning."[18]

Discovering the connections is, in the end, what the Basic School curriculum is all about.

Measuring Results

> *The Basic School is accountable to parents, to students, and to the community at large. Academic standards are established both in language and the Core Commonalities, with benchmarks to monitor student achievement. The personal and social qualities of students also are observed and evaluated informally by teachers. Assessment in the Basic School is, always, in the service of learning.*

The Basic School is an accountable institution, accountable to parents, to students, and to the larger community. Children go to school month after month and everyone involved, including those who fund public education, has a legitimate right to know what learning has occurred. "Standards and assessment represent a cornerstone of education reform," said educator and historian Diane Ravitch. "Without them, it's very difficult to have a sense of what you're trying to accomplish."[1]

As a first step, Basic Schools participate in district or state assessment programs with full confidence in the ability of their students to achieve. But assessment in the Basic School is linked directly to instruction. It is an essential part of teaching, and every effort is made to assure that what is measured flows from what is taught. Grant Wiggins, whose work focuses on assessment, said it this way: "Good teaching is inseparable from good assessing." The question, therefore, is not whether to evaluate students, but how to measure performance in ways that will enrich learning, rather than restrict it.

SETTING THE STANDARDS

Assessment begins with goals, with a clear sense of what each student is expected to accomplish. And the Basic School has two goals that relate directly to academic achievement—*proficiency in language* and the acquisition of a *core of knowledge*. Three other goals have to do with the personal and social qualities of students—motivation, social and emotional well-being, and responsible living.

These five goals, taken together, provide the framework for assessment in the Basic School, and each goal requires appropriate, sensitive evaluation, but in different ways.

Measuring Literacy. The first goal—*proficiency in language*—calls for careful evaluation of student achievement in English, mathematics, *and* the arts. The school must know, as a key component of assessment, that each student is becoming linguistically empowered. For this to be accomplished, goals must be developed for all three forms of language. The following illustrates what we have in mind:

· In *verbal literacy*, each student develops skills and confidence in the use of spoken and written English, becoming capable of sending clear, effective messages, and of receiving, with understanding and discernment, verbal communication from others.

·   In *mathematical literacy*, each student develops skills and confidence in the use of numbers, understanding and applying mathematical concepts with accuracy, solving problems, and appreciating the aesthetic characteristics of mathematics.

·   In *artistic literacy*, each student develops skills and confidence in the language of the arts, learning to look and listen with sensitivity and intelligence, and, at a basic level, to be self-expressive in music, drama, dance, and the visual arts.

Having established goals, the next step is to define the *achievement standards*, as well as *benchmarks*, making it possible to track, periodically, the language proficiency of each student. Some Basic Schools may define their own standards. Others may use those mandated by the district or the state. Still others may adopt voluntary standards being developed nationwide. The important point is for each Basic School to know clearly what standards to apply in monitoring student progress in *literacy* over the course of six years.

Measuring Core Knowledge. The second goal is to help each student acquire a core of essential knowledge, which, in the Basic School, is organized around integrative themes called the Core Commonalities. Here again, what's required first are clearly defined *goals*— with expected *outcomes*—for each of the eight commonalities that provide the curriculum framework for the Basic School.

While studying the Life Cycle, it is expected that children will learn about their bodies and how human life is nurtured and sustained. In Connections to Nature, students learn about the natural world, about how all life forms relate to each other, and how the scientific method opens up the world for intensive exploration. We also define goals for the other commonalities.

In addition to clear goals, each commonality will also have well-defined and measurable *achievement standards*, along with detailed *benchmarks*, based on the content to be studied. Such standards and benchmarks make it possible for teachers to monitor student achievement incrementally, and match learning experiences to individual needs. "The primary reason for formal assessment tasks," states the North Dakota Study Group on Evaluation, "is to find out what each child knows and can do in a specific content area on a certain date."[2]

In the early grades, the general knowledge assessment program we have just described is *embedded* in each lesson plan. Instruction and evaluation go together. At the end of the fourth grade, however, the Basic School will introduce a *summative assessment* to measure the student's cumulative knowledge and understanding on several levels.

·   First, the summative assessment will measure the student's *acquisition of a core of essential knowledge* in the traditional academic fields, such as history, civics, literature, and science.

·   Second, it will measure *the ability of students to integrate* what has been learned.

· Third, it will measure the students' *capacity to apply* what they have learned and relate classroom instruction to real-life issues.

Measuring Personal Growth. Beyond the two *academic* goals of literacy and general knowledge, the Basic School has three other goals for students: *to be well motivated, to have a sense of well-being*, and *to live responsibly.* These goals, while also critically important, are not "measured" formally in the Basic School, for two reasons: First, as things now stand, educators simply do not have good ways to evaluate, with any degree of objectivity, personal and social qualities. It is difficult, for example, to establish quantitative benchmarks for "motivation" or "social well-being." Second, to measure selected personal characteristics in isolation ignores the fact that social and emotional and ethical qualities are inseparably related to the whole life of the child.

Still, while the personal and social characteristics of students will not be conventionally assessed, they are not neglected. The Basic School does define "core virtues" and standards of conduct. And teachers, as an ongoing part of instruction, observe and encourage each student, by word and example, to move toward higher standards.

In the end, the aim of assessment in the Basic School is to assure that all five goals—*literacy, general knowledge, motivation, sense of well-being,* and *responsible living*—have been satisfactorily met by all students, since both the mastery of academic content *and* the development of good character are the ultimate purposes of the Basic School.

GATHERING THE EVIDENCE

In the Basic School, the evidence used to evaluate students is gathered from a variety of sources, using what some have called the "portfolio approach." A "portfolio" is not only a place to put things, it is also a reminder that in assessing students the sources of evidence should be rich and varied.

One elementary school we visited received six hundred new pizza boxes donated by a local supermarket, and these served as "portfolios" for student work. Regardless of the name—or the container—what's important to remember is that, in student evaluation, a broad range of evidence should be used and that the sampling of student work should be gathered over time.

First, written responses. In assessing academic progress, schools traditionally have asked students to give paper-and-pencil answers to carefully constructed questions. This evidence does have a place in the Basic School, with the clear understanding that such assessment seems most appropriate for the upper grades and again should relate to school goals—to what is being taught.

By answering multiple-choice and other short-answer questions, a student can reveal knowledge of a subject, the level of his or her discrete skills, as well as an understanding of basic concepts and ideas. Written examinations are especially helpful in measuring student achievement in English and mathematics. Specifically, grammar and computation skills can be recorded quickly and efficiently, with progress noted over time.

In a study of sixty-one teachers in eighteen elementary schools in New York City, researchers found a wide variety of written forms of evidence being used, ranging from writing samples, letters, and children's journals with drawings, to book summaries, essay reports, worksheets, notebooks, and sentence starters. The teachers reported using such evidence not only to evaluate students, but also to inform themselves about their instructional strategies within the classroom.[3] The key, teachers felt, was accumulating and looking at written work over time.

The same applies to math. At the Sandyhook Elementary School in New Town, Connecticut, teachers have developed their own standard paper-and-pencil tests for mathematics. But while the form looks familiar, the questions are often open-ended, requiring students to write responses, with no emphasis on speed. "We are teaching the children that thinking takes time, and that good thinking is valuable," explained Wendy Foreman, math teacher.

Student achievement in the arts, although more difficult to measure perhaps, also should be systematically evaluated. Again, Howard Gardner, in *Frames of Mind*, reminds us that beyond linguistic intelligence and logical-mathematical skills, students also have artistic intelligences.[4] This intelligence is neglected when teachers feel uncertain about how to assess artistic work. Thus, in the Basic School, every effort is made to establish measurement standards and benchmarks in the arts.

It is possible to assess proficiency in the arts, including using written responses, that promote both creativity and solid achievement. In the Pittsburgh schools, Arts PROPEL is an arts curriculum that includes thoughtful and systematic written evaluations. Students are given carefully constructed exercises as they produce a work of art that involves *production*, *perception*, and *reflection*. Students then write a critique of their own work, and also of each other's work, using agreed-upon standards. Final evaluation stresses both process and finished product.[5]

Second, teacher observation. In the Basic School, teachers are viewed as the best source of evaluation. Teachers are, after all, with students every day and are, continuously, putting bits of evidence together, picking up important clues. In fact, the word "assess" is derived from the Latin word "assidere," meaning "to sit beside."[6]

An experienced, insightful teacher can, without question, provide the most accurate, most revealing portrait of student growth. But a teacher's skill in evaluating students doesn't just happen. It must be learned. And in the Basic School, staff development includes seminars on how to gather evidence and monitor, effectively, the progress of every student.

One approach teachers use to gather evidence is often referred to as *narrative notations.* Using this method, teachers observe and write down, in an open-ended fashion, significant events that mark student progress, and reveal either growth or barriers to learning. Such information may be gathered while a group of students works together on a science project, or as a student works independently, or with a computer. Narrative notations are not randomly selected observations. Rather, goals and standards and benchmarks always are kept in mind.

At the New Suncook School in Lovell, Maine, narrative notations are used by teachers who work together. While observing students individually or in groups, teachers record, in writing, each child's performance. The school developed anecdotal reporting tools to involve parents, as well. These include what's called

Magic Moments Books, in which the teacher records "proud moments" of achievement, and sends the book home for parents to write down significant moments in their child's learning. Such observations become part of the formal assessment records.

Teachers may also use a more structured approach called the *observational checklist*, which is especially appropriate for recording incremental development of discrete skills. Here, the teacher checks off student performance as measured against a list of preestablished standards and benchmarks. In mathematics, for example, the checklist might include the fundamentals of computation. In the arts, teachers might record the student's developing ability to play an instrument, or create a finished work of art, or act on stage before an audience. In verbal language, student participation in group discussion or more formal speech-making might be recorded. This checklist also becomes part of the portfolio.

We cannot stress strongly enough that, in the Basic School, *performance-based* information relates, always, to clearly defined standards and benchmarks and that observations are reported in a sharply focused manner. This approach to assessment, while time consuming, is often praised by teachers precisely because it links evaluation directly to student learning and provides a richer, more revealing profile of student progress.

Samuel J. Meisels, a national leader in assessment and professor at the University of Michigan, states that performance-based assessment "enables students to demonstrate their knowledge or skills through solving problems, doing mathematical computations, writing journal entries or essays, conducting experiments, presenting oral reports, or assembling a portfolio of representative work."[7]

In a third-grade classroom at Gibson Elementary School in Clark County, Nevada, the teacher watched students solve problems using concrete objects, such as stones, in a mathematics examination, and systematically recorded observations. Misunderstandings were uncovered that had been missed when students worked only with abstract numbers. The performance-based assessment revealed, for example, that only six of the forty-five students really understood "place value," even though many more than six had scored well on a conventional paper-and-pencil test.

Third, student products and performance. In the Basic School, assessment also includes the creative products and performances of students which go beyond the well-known written tests or even teacher notes. Essays, book reports, journal entries, letters, all reveal a student's proficiency in literacy, which is perhaps the single most important evidence in measuring academic progress. Audiotapes of student reports, readings, and recitations are also useful in documenting language progress over time.

During school visits, we were impressed by just how much time young children spend *making things*, working with their hands—shaping clay objects, painting, drawing, building birdhouses, or conducting a science experiment. Evidence from these creative activities also reveals student growth and demonstrates achievement. When students make bulky objects too large for the portfolio, photographs or a videotape of the completed project may be used. But, here again, samples for evaluation should be selected and critiqued carefully, using well-defined standards.

While visiting the Irving Weber Elementary School in Iowa City, Iowa, we observed that fourth-graders had taken paper-and-pencil tests to measure the knowledge they acquired from a study of the rain forest, an integrated unit that focused on "Connections to Nature." Through multiple-choice questions, essays, and fill-in-the-blank answers, students were evaluated on their knowledge in several disciplines, including geography, science, and history. But evaluation of this fourth-grade class also included a nine- by twenty-foot rain forest mural the students had constructed which had three-dimensional paper monkeys, beetles, spiders, colorful birds, broad-leafed vegetation, all scaled to size. The mural demonstrated students' mathematical and artistic skills, as well as knowledge of the rain forest's ecosystem.

Theater production touches yet another dimension of student achievement that might be assessed. It's hard to put a recital or a theater performance in a portfolio. But again such activities can be videotaped and become part of the student's record. Teachers at the Key School in Indianapolis pioneered the use of "video portfolios" eight years ago. Videos vividly reveal the child's strengths and weaknesses in oral language and provide evidence of student progress.

Fourth, parent and student information. Finally, parents and students in the Basic School are partners in evaluation. Research shows that parents who receive frequent and positive messages about assessment are more likely to talk to their child about school work and monitor progress.[8] They can, for example, discuss the child's study habits and contribute their own impressions. This means, of course, that parents must be fully informed about the school's goals. Parents also may be asked to record their own observations of student learning at home, in reading, for example, or in oral language, or the arts.

In the Basic School, students, too, are asked to step back and assess their own learning, to reflect orally or in writing on their work. They might be asked: "How do you feel about your progress in mathematics?" "What do you believe are your stronger areas?" "What problems do you think you need to tackle now?" Involving students in assessment actively engages them in their own education and dispels the perception that assessment is a "game of gotcha."

In England, some schools now include students as part of the parent-teacher conference sessions. It becomes a time to have a three-way conversation about goals and progress, and to address small problems as they occur. The conferences, originally called "Parent Consultation Days," have been renamed "Student Review Days" to make the point that the student is the focus.

At Rolling Hill Elementary School in Fairfax County, Virginia, teachers, students, and the principal engage in "portfolio conferences." Students are prepared for these meetings during classroom discussions, and they are consulted on a variety of questions such as: "What skills are shown by the writing in your portfolio?" "Do the mathematics papers show progress?" "Why?" At the first reporting period in November, parents meet with the teacher and discuss the contents of their child's portfolio. The portfolio then goes home so children and parents can analyze it together. Evaluation at Rolling Hill is a tool to enrich learning, and parents and students are partners in the process.

Last fall, we observed one kindergarten teacher preparing for an early November parent conference. She reviewed her notes about each child and looked again at the written work, at the test results, and at the collection of drawings and paintings in the portfolio. The teacher then listed questions she wanted to ask the parent. "I always know and understand more about the children after the conferences . . . and it's important to keep parents informed," she said. "Through it all, children should be growing, responsibly, and with enthusiasm, toward high standards. My goal is to assure that no child be allowed to fail."

MEASURING THE SCHOOL

In the Basic School, evaluation is a process that focuses, ultimately, on the school itself. All members of the community pause occasionally to consider what actions the school is taking to implement, in its own distinctive way, the four priorities of the Basic School—from building community to building character. We suggest, specifically, that local school board members, the principal, teachers, and parents meet, at least once a year, to talk about how their school is doing.

The Basic School community might then prepare a *school* report card organized around the key components, drawing a profile of its strengths and weaknesses *as community*. Important questions to be addressed might include: Is our Basic School a community with clear goals? Are teachers leaders? Are parents active partners in the school program? Is language viewed as central to all learning? Is there a core curriculum? Are there clear achievement standards, with various sources used for measuring student success? Are there flexible grouping arrangements? Is there a rich array of learning resources? Are children's physical, emotional, and social needs met? Does the school emphasize character as well as competence?

In the end, the goal of assessment in the Basic School is not only to strengthen community but, above all, to enrich the climate for learning and extend, for all students, their prospects for success. James Agee wrote: "In every child who is born, under no matter what circumstances, of no matter what parents, the potentiality of the human race is born again."[9] In the Basic School, "measuring results" means finding authentic ways to affirm and strengthen the potential of every child.

A CLIMATE FOR LEARNING

Patterns to Fit Purpose

> *In the Basic School, every student is encouraged to become a disciplined, creative, well-motivated learner. Class size is kept small, the teaching schedule is flexible, and student grouping arrangements are varied to promote learning. Connections are made across the generations, to strengthen community and enrich the lives of students.*

On a warm April afternoon, we walked unannounced into a fifth-grade classroom in New Haven, Connecticut. Thirty students were crowded around the teacher's desk, not sitting in orderly rows. Was this a friendly scene, or had something ominous occurred? Pausing, we discovered a magic moment. These streetwise children were discussing Charles Dickens' *Oliver Twist*, debating, with great enthusiasm, whether little Oliver could survive in their own home town. They concluded that, while Oliver had survived in far-off London, he'd never make it in New Haven, a much tougher city.

The Basic School is, first, a *community* with shared goals. Second, it has a *curriculum with coherence*. The third priority brings it all together in a *climate* that promotes learning. Such a climate, like the classroom we encountered in New Haven, is sparked by

TABLE 17

HOW DO ELEMENTARY STUDENTS FEEL ABOUT THEIR TEACHERS?

	PERCENTAGE OF STUDENTS AGREEING
Most of the teachers I have had in this school are good.	96%
If I do poorly at school work, my teachers encourage me to do better.	96
Almost all the teachers in my school care a lot about children.	96
My teachers usually want to hear my ideas.	91

SOURCE: The Carnegie Foundation for the Advancement of Teaching and the George H. Gallup International Institute, The International Schooling Project, 1994 (United States).

great teachers who perform heroic acts every day, often working under difficult conditions.

This nation has always been ambivalent about teachers. "[R]eal regard shown those who taught has never matched the professed regard," is the way professor Dan Lortie, at the University of Chicago, put it.[1] It's true that not all teachers are effective. Still, during school visits, the vast majority of teachers we observed were committed, creative, and—we discovered—well liked by their students. Indeed, more than 90 percent of the elementary students we surveyed agreed that most of their teachers are "good." They also agreed, overwhelmingly, that teachers encourage them "to do better," "want to hear their ideas," and "care a lot about children" (table 17).

With all the talk about school problems, we should celebrate the fact that elementary school students in this country feel so good about their teachers.

When all is said and done, excellence in education means excellence in teaching. But for teachers fully to succeed, classroom conditions must improve, beginning with smaller classes, especially in the early grades. The daily class schedule must be more flexible. Students should be grouped in a variety of ways, and schools should make connections across the generations. Simply stated, the *patterns for learning* in the Basic School are organized to fit purpose.

CLASS SIZE TO FIT PURPOSE

For about six hours every day, students and teachers live in classrooms not much larger than a spacious living room. Each student occupies a few feet of space, and this does not take into account desks, tables, and chairs. Classrooms are filled, and often overfilled, with children. Most adults would have their hands full taking care of only four or five young children for hours every day. Yet primary school classes in this country have, on average, about twenty-five students (table 18). When we surveyed kindergarten teachers a few years ago, we found some classes with *forty-one* children![2] And then we talk about being world class in education.

One fall day, we visited a Midwest elementary school where thirty children were crowded into one small room. Desks were pushed close together. We found it difficult to move from one work station to another, and it was almost impossible for the teacher to give students individual attention. About twenty minutes of every hour ended up being devoted to distractions, not to teaching and learning. At the end of the hectic day, the teacher

TABLE 18

AVERAGE CLASS SIZE OF U.S. ELEMENTARY SCHOOLS

	MEAN NUMBER OF STUDENTS
Kindergarten	23
First grade	24
Second grade	24
Third grade	25
Fourth grade	26

SOURCE: The Carnegie Foundation for the Advancement of Teaching, National Survey of Elementary School Principals, 1990.

said: "When someone says to me class size doesn't matter, I know they've never spent a full day or even an hour with thirty-five six-year-olds."

Small classes do enrich learning, especially in the primary grades. This is a time when children develop physically and intellectually at very different rates, when they need personal attention, not only to promote learning, but also to track down lost gloves and boots. The simple truth is that young children, to be most successful in learning, at least occasionally need one-on-one attention. And if this nation is serious about high academic achievement for all students, perhaps the most important investment we could make would be to reduce class size in the early grades.

A Tennessee study revealed that when class size was restricted to seventeen, students in small classes outperformed, in all subjects, those in larger ones.[3] A statewide program in Indiana called "Prime Time" reduced class size to twenty or fewer students in the early grades, with positive results.[4] Further, a recent Gallup poll revealed that 82 percent of public school parents surveyed agree that small classes make "a great deal of difference."[5] What's alarming, however, is that budget cuts are moving some schools in precisely the opposite direction.

A reasonable class size is, without question, key to excellence in the early grades. And for the Basic School, we recommend that the class size be limited, ideally, to no more than seventeen, surely no more than twenty students each. For many schools this may mean more teachers and more money, an investment that unquestionably will pay off. The real issue, however, is the ratio of adults to children. Some schools we visited were using university interns, or parents and grandparents, as teacher aides, to give all youngsters close and continuing attention.

Small classes, while important, are not sufficient. The way classrooms are physically arranged also sends an important message to students. One classroom we visited in North Carolina had small tables placed strategically around the room, with "work stations"—a science lab, a computer center, a garden space. In the corner there was a "Reading Nest," with a raised platform covered with pillows. An area carpet was in the center and splashes of artwork, maps, and large printed posters covered the walls. In this classroom, the focus clearly was on learning, not on the teacher's desk.

In the Basic School, there is no rigid formula. Outstanding teachers can function effectively in a variety of settings. The goal should be to arrange the room in ways that will enhance learning, encourage group interaction, and give to children a sense of beauty and order. In the end, the teacher must decide.

RESETTING THE CLOCK

Time is the student's treasure. Work that is truly valued takes time, and to expect a child to complete artwork in twenty-minute intervals, twice a week, or to complete a science experiment or write a poem or story in thirty minutes is, of course, foolish. More than 90 percent of the elementary school principals surveyed said that teachers should have "flexibility" in organizing the school day.[6] We agree.

We found, however, that in far too many schools, the day is chopped up in ways that restrict learning. Units of study are forced into blocks of time. One teacher observed flatly: "The day is too fragmented for the kind of learning I want. Having "time blocks" has nothing to do with how I want to teach, or how children learn." A third-grade teacher in Illinois told us: "We always are driven by a rigid schedule. We laugh a little about it, but the truth is the clock is ticking off rigid periods. It is one of the most oppressive features of teaching at our school."

The school day must, of course, be planned. Teachers, as they think about the day, must carefully consider just how much time will be devoted to various lessons. Such scheduling should, however, serve only as a guide, not a mandate. In the Basic School, time is in the service of learning. Specifically, we recommend that teachers in each classroom be free to adjust the class schedule and be held accountable for results, not their conformity to the clock.

GROUPING TO FIT PURPOSE

One of the most controversial issues we encountered was how students should be "grouped"—with some teachers and parents supporting the so-called "graded" classroom and others advocating "nongraded" grouping. One teacher said: "Frankly, I'm convinced that the structured grade level should be abandoned to make way for a system that is more developmentally oriented." Others worry about too much openness. A teacher in a "nongraded" school complained: "It doesn't make sense to put five- and eight-year-olds together all day when their attention spans and levels of learning readiness are so different."

In earlier days, students went to one- or two-room schoolhouses where everyone was grouped together, and where older students often taught the younger ones. The "graded" school—placing students in classrooms based on age—became popular in the late nineteenth century as enrollments grew and as schools needed to become organizationally more "efficient."[7] Rigid time blocks and grouping arrangements soon became standardized, creating what some have called "the factory model."

Albert Shanker, president of the American Federation of Teachers, asks the key question: "How do we organize schools and classrooms, given the fact that kids learn differently and at different rates?"[8] Perhaps students should be mastering material and moving ahead without grade-level restrictions. Otherwise, an enthusiasm for learning may be stifled at an early age.

Clearly, the time has come to move beyond the tired old "graded versus nongraded" debate—just one more false dichotomy in education. What is needed, we believe, is a more *flexible* approach to grouping. In the Basic School, students are grouped in at least five different ways, reflecting the fact that "kids do learn differently and at different rates," as Mr. Shanker put it. Specifically, we recommend for every Basic School:

- · *homeroom grouping*, for placement and a sense of family;
- · *mixed-age grouping*, for cooperative learning;
- · *focused grouping*, for intensive coaching;
- · *individual grouping*, for independent study;
- · *all-school grouping*, for community building.

Homeroom Grouping. In the Basic School, we begin, first, with the homeroom. By "homeroom," we mean grouping students initially by age, for a home base. Since birthdays determine when children enroll in school, putting students in a class based on age makes sense administratively, and it's a procedure parents understand. Even more important, homerooms also can give to each child a sense of "family"—a place where children begin and end each day, and in the early grades the homeroom is the place where students do a lot of learning, too.

Some Basic Schools may wish to break out of the "single-age" homeroom and place children of different ages, such as five- and six-year-olds, together. Others may wish to keep a homeroom together, with one teacher, for more than a single year. Researchers Edward A. Wynne and Herbert J. Walberg, after studying student grouping both here and overseas, concluded that the effectiveness of learning in American schools is often tempered because children and teachers are together for only a year, as a rule.

They believe that "schools should try to keep discrete groups of students and teachers together over long periods of time."[9]

At Waldorf Schools, an international network of independent institutions, students stay with a "main teacher" for eight years. An intimate, supportive learning community is established. At Seminole Springs Elementary School in Eustis, Florida, students and teachers stay together for educational *and* social reasons for as long as three years. "In our country, the family is not as strong as it once was," said principal Jack Currie. "For those kids who don't have a strong mom-and-dad model, the teacher becomes a significant other."[10] Keeping the group together builds confidence and caring.

Regardless of the length of time together, Basic School students most frequently are placed, first, in a homeroom, based on age.

Mixed-age Grouping. In the Basic School, the homeroom is not an isolated island; it's a staging ground for action. Far from being cut off from other classes, teachers and students in each homeroom regularly work with those in other classrooms, not just at their own level but at other grade levels, too. Fourth-graders and kindergartners, for example, meet together on a science project, while fifth-graders help first-graders with reading or mathematics lessons. Such mixed-age grouping has powerful benefits, both educationally and socially.

By mentoring children in a lower grade, older students develop a sense of responsibility. Younger children, on the other hand, feel more secure as they get to know "a bigger kid." Further, researcher Robert Slavin reports that "cooperative learning" across grade levels is a key component to successful education. In a program called "Success for All," which has spread nationwide from Baltimore, older students tutor younger ones, demonstrating also that such grouping develops both language and social skills.[11]

Mixing the ages works especially well in the Basic School, with its thematic curriculum that spirals upward—making it possible for first-graders and fifth-graders to work together on such themes as the Life Cycle and Connections to Nature. Older students can teach younger ones about good health and safety habits, and in so doing, teach themselves. It also works the other way. In one school where the Core Commonalities curriculum is being used, we overheard a second-grader telling a fourth-grader what it means to "produce and consume."

Students at Ridgeway Elementary School in Columbia, Missouri, have "Learning Communities" that span two grade levels, with three or four teachers in each community. Teachers believe these mixed-age communities have contributed to the academic achievement of their students. They point out that 97 percent of Ridgeway's former students, including those diagnosed as "learning disabled," were on the junior high honor roll after they moved on. Two Ridgeway students were Presidential Scholars in high school.

"We've learned that chronological age doesn't mean everything in terms of learning," notes Susan Fales, the principal. "In our school, you may have seventy to eighty kids interacting with each other on many levels—academic and social—and they clearly spark each other. The focus is on individual success, *within community*—not a single age or grade."

Focused Grouping. As a third approach, Basic School students with similar aptitudes and interests occasionally are brought together for intensive coaching, an arrangement we've called "focused grouping." Small groups of students concentrate on a special task, skill, or project within a class or across grade levels. The value of such an approach seems apparent. Consider sports: Typically, beginners in tennis are placed in one group, the more advanced in another. In music, beginning piano players do not routinely receive lessons with more proficient players.

Similarly, focused grouping can be helpful in academic learning, too—in reading and writing, mathematics and science, for example. Children who need intensive coaching in one area or another should get it—and those with common interests also should be encouraged to meet together.

At the Key School in Indianapolis, students are organized into special interest groups, called "pods," that meet four times each week. Math, architecture, drama, choir, instrumental music, and the physical sciences are among the offerings. Specialists teach the violin or a foreign language. In the "math pod," students play board games that develop their logical, spatial, and mathematical skills. In the "architecture pod," students with special interests adopt houses in the neighborhood, present reports on them, and go on architectural walking tours.

Focused grouping can, without question, be pedagogically effective. As students with similar interests and skills work together, they gain confidence and encourage one another. But we add a strong word of caution: In the Basic School, focused grouping is *always* a temporary arrangement. Under no circumstances are students to be "tracked," locked rigidly into a class or group that separates them, based on an arbitrary judgment. The Johns Hopkins University researchers report that homogeneous grouping can, in fact, be effective *when it is integrated in the course of a day with other arrangements.*

Individual Grouping. Many times, throughout the day and week, students in the Basic School also engage in independent study— in an arrangement we call "individual grouping." Working on their own in a classroom or in the school's Learning Resource Center, they gather evidence, write reports, or complete an experiment on a challenging math assignment. Just as a musician must occasionally practice alone, students, too, need time alone to concentrate on a single task, developing skills in independent study.

Individual grouping can also be used for students who need intensive one-on-one assistance, either from a teacher, an aide, or a parent volunteer, and for children with special needs who require extra guidance and support.

In one school in the Midwest, we walked into a classroom mid-day, and the teacher met us at the door. All students were deeply engaged in self-guided projects. They hardly noticed our arrival. We moved easily from one work station to another, observing one student at a computer writing a story, another checking an experiment, a third reading silently in a corner, all completing their own projects, without distractions.

At another school we visited, the day begins with a fifteen-minute silent reading period. Everyone in the school—the principal, teachers, students, secretaries, and the custodian—sits quietly and reads when the bell rings at 8:15 A.M. The principal announces over the public address system: "DEAR Time—Drop Everything and Read." Each day begins in a climate of concentrated, self-directed learning.

All-school Grouping. While all students study on their own, there are times when the *whole school* becomes a classroom, when everyone in the Basic School has a shared experience. On such occasions, children in the fifth-grade read their poetry to others, or a third-grade class puts on a play for the entire school, or student musicians, from across grade levels, present a concert. In the Basic School, such celebrative gatherings are scheduled regularly throughout the year. The point of these all-school groupings is, as educator Theodore Sizer elegantly put it, "the gathering of children"—a time to affirm the school as a community for learning.

At the Cambridge Friends School in Massachusetts, everyone comes together every Thursday morning. On the day we were there, students and teachers were joined by parents in the modest-sized gymnasium. Everyone sat on the floor. A performance by third-graders—with African drum music and Japanese dances—began the celebration, with the audience in rapt attention. Hearty applause followed each presentation. Next, a kindergarten teacher led everyone singing, *"If you had potatoes and I had tomatoes, we could have dinner together,"* and *"You know I'd be glad to share what I had, cause that's what friends are for."* Kindergartners were thrilled, of course, and third- and fourth-graders participated wholeheartedly, too. Over two hundred students swayed, sang together, supporting one another, meeting as one class.

CONNECTIONS ACROSS THE GENERATIONS

Finally, grouping patterns in the Basic School extend outward, beyond the school itself, to include parents and grandparents. The school brings the generations together at a time when "children are growing up alone," as one kindergarten teacher told us. "I think it's really sad," she said, "that youngsters never seem to be with older people these days. They don't know how adults think or what they do. I'm convinced it affects their learning." Another said: "It's not healthy for young children to be so isolated. They need to learn lessons from the older generation."

In America today, older and younger people exist side by side, brushing elbows but hardly touching one another. Toddlers are in day care, and older children are in school, often organized rigidly by age. Young adults go off to college, parents are in the workplace, older people are in retirement villages, nursing homes, or apartments, living all alone. What we are left with is a "horizontal culture," one in which each age group is disconnected from the others, and it's possible, quite literally, to go through life spending most waking hours only with one's peers.

Psychiatrist James P. Comer, in reflecting on his own childhood, concluded that much of the trouble we attribute to our young really stems from their sense of separation from the larger world. When he was growing up, Dr. Comer says, adults were "locked into a conspiracy" of protection for a child.[12] "And children knew what to expect . . . ," he said. "[E]veryone had a real sense of place and belonging. Even if you didn't have high status, you really had a sense of community. . . . Everything a child knew about what was right and wrong, good and bad, came to him or her through those adult authority figures. Now we may not think of that as so desirable; on the other hand, those young people felt supported by the adults who could sanction or not sanction behavior."[13]

"The continuity of all cultures depends on the living presence of at least three generations," wrote anthropologist Margaret Mead.[14] Quality education requires such relationships as well. And in the Basic School, bridges are built to connect the generations. Specifically, we propose intergenerational grouping programs, with retirement villages becoming classrooms and with older people serving as mentors and tutors to young students through "Grandteacher" programs.

Researchers at the University of Pittsburgh found that student performance improves in mathematics, reading, spelling, grammar, English language, and even handwriting when senior citizens help in classrooms. Further, when teachers were asked to evaluate the impact older people had, they overwhelmingly reported improvements in the psychological well-being of students, such as "motivation to learn" and "less aggressive behavior." In addition, participation by an older person freed teachers to give individual students more attention (table 19).[15]

Last fall, students at David Cox Road School in Charlotte, North Carolina, traveled by bus to the local nursing home. Seniors gathered to hear the children sing "The World Is a Rainbow," and, at the end, applauded, calling for encores. In the lounge, materials for pumpkin painting were set up and seniors in wheelchairs, joined by the children, sat around the tables. On the second floor, several seniors, though ambulatory, rarely left their

TABLE 19

HOW TEACHERS VIEW THE IMPACT OF
OLDER PEOPLE IN THE CLASSROOM
(PERCENTAGE AGREEING)

	MORE COMMON	NO CHANGE	LESS COMMON
IMPACT ON STUDENTS			
Students motivated to learn	82%	17%	0%
Cooperative student behavior	79	20	0
Positive student behavior	76	21	0
Students relaxed/contented	68	29	0
Aggressive student behavior	7	53	35
IMPACT ON TEACHERS			
Teacher time to work with individuals or small groups	78	22	0
Teacher time to work with large student groups or whole class	55	39	4
Teacher insight into student behavior	54	44	1

SOURCE: Sally Newman and Julie Riess, "Older Workers in Intergenerational Child Care," *Generations Together*, July 1990, 18.

beds, but a staff member took several children to each room personally to invite the seniors, who then left their beds for the first time in months. Later, as the children departed, residents cried. The children gave assurances that they'd be back. Joy Warner, a teacher at the school, told us, "Children learn best when they interact with others, seeing beauty in all kinds of people, and learning how to give."[16]

In the Basic School, every learning pattern fits a purpose. Classes are *small* enough for teachers to give students one-on-one instruction. The class schedule is *flexible* enough to support creative teaching. Student grouping patterns are *varied* enough to enrich learning, and the classroom is *open* enough to encourage connections across the generations. Linda Darling-Hammond, professor at Teachers College, Columbia University, expressed it well: "The challenge is to focus on what students need and then work in an environment flexible enough to allow us to meet those needs."[17]

Resources to Enrich

> *The Basic School makes available to all students rich resources for learning, from building blocks to books. Libraries, zoos, museums, and parks in the surrounding community become resources, too. And on the threshold of a new century, the Basic School gives students access to the new electronic tools that connect each classroom to vast networks of knowledge.*

In Amy Natiello's fifth-grade classroom at Orchard School in Ridgewood, New Jersey, we found bookshelves with such classics as *Robinson Crusoe* and *The Adventures of Tom Sawyer*, and more recent award-winning books such as *Shiloh*, by Phyllis Reynolds Naylor and *A Wrinkle in Time*, by Madeleine L'Engle. There were maps, a globe, and a "grow lab" for garden plants. But the classroom also had computers, a CD-ROM, a cable TV monitor, and a telephone. Using these electronic tools, students were mastering math concepts and writing creatively. And they were even working collaboratively with students in New Zealand to study acid rain using the National Geographic computer network.

VCRS, computers, and laser discs can, without question, transform the classroom and dramatically enrich learning.

137

Ms. Natiello put the challenge this way: "If you're an educator, and a conscientious learner, how can you ignore technology? It's all around us. To me it's exciting to make these remarkable tools work for children and watch them enrich my class."

The Basic School is resource rich, a place with books, art supplies, garden space, a neighborhood for learning, and technology that, quite literally, connects students to resources all around the world. Consider how a fourth-grader sitting in a classroom in New Jersey or in Oregon or in Ohio can take a "magic carpet" field trip to the Smithsonian Institution in Washington, D.C. Consider, too, how it's now possible for young students to be electronically "transported" to the moon or to the bottom of the sea, or to peer inside a human cell.

But, frankly, it's foolish to talk about CD-ROMs—or taking magic carpet trips—in schools where textbooks are out of date and paper and pencils are in short supply. One teacher in a small school in Missouri noted: "Our school board keeps talking about computers. This is so ironic since almost every weekend I go out and get a new supply of crayons, paste, and construction paper simply because we have no supplies budgeted at the school." A first-grade teacher in suburban Arizona said: "I was given two boxes of paper last winter and told that's it for the year. A good portion of my paycheck buys things for our room—paper, pencils, crayons, the basics. Heaven help us!"

According to teachers we surveyed, nearly half report that their schools do not have adequate reference books, science materials, or sports equipment. More than one in four do not have adequate books and instructional materials, and fully a third of the teachers

TABLE 20

ARE THE FOLLOWING INSTRUCTIONAL RESOURCES
IN ADEQUATE SUPPLY?

	PERCENTAGE OF TEACHERS INDICATING "HAVE ENOUGH/IS AVAILABLE"
Paper and pencils	77%
Books and instructional materials	73
Audio-visual equipment	67
School library	64
Maps	60
Art supplies	55
Science materials	49
Sports equipment	46
Classroom reference books	46

SOURCE: The Carnegie Foundation for the Advancement of Teaching and the George H. Gallup International Institute, The International Schooling Project, 1994 (United States).

rated the school library as inadequate. More than 20 percent said paper and pencils were in short supply at their school (table 20). What's most disturbing is that teachers in this country actually spend hundreds of dollars of their own money every year to buy school supplies.[1]

In the Basic School, resources for learning begin, then, with the essentials—paper and pencils, maps, globes, microscopes, art supplies, and even building blocks, which can, as author Joanne Oppenheim notes, "become a skyscraper today, a zoo tomorrow, and a space station the next day." Classrooms in Basic Schools are also well stocked with modeling clay, rock collections, tape measures and weigh scales, and perhaps fish, a gerbil or two, and garden space, all of which excite children and invite discovery.

The Craycroft Elementary School in Tucson, Arizona, turned its barren school yard into a desert habitat, with a meandering trail one quarter of a mile long that passed by cactus and rocks and desert animals. A seemingly dead space became a living laboratory. Craycroft also created garden spaces—outdoor classrooms where students planted seedlings. Railroad ties, donated by the Southern Pacific Railroad, line the garden rows. There's also a fish pond, a waterfall, and a marsh area where students make soil comparisons and analyze the water's nutrients, learning lessons in Connections to Nature. A three-hundred-gallon collection tank takes the runoff from the school roof to irrigate the garden soil.

In the Basic School, hands-on resources are basic to all learning.

A TREASURY OF BOOKS

In the Basic School, books are everywhere. Reading is celebrated in every classroom. And rather than offering only "basal readers," every classroom is stocked with classics. Children learn to treasure E. B. White's *Charlotte's Web*, Maurice Sendak's *Where the Wild Things Are*, Hans Christian Andersen's *The Emperor's New Clothes* and *The Nightingale*, and Mildred Taylor's *Roll of Thunder, Hear My Cry*, to name a few such treasures.

Each Basic School also has, ideally, a Learning Resource Center— a "classroom for all classes," as one third-grade teacher described it. Not only does the center serve as a treasure-trove of books, it

has recordings, videotapes, and computer programs which enhance learning. There is, in fact, a direct correlation between
students' achievement and the size of a school library or media
center, according to a recent Colorado study.[2]

At a modestly funded school in the Southeast, we discovered an
old library that had been transformed into a bright and spacious
resource room, carpeted throughout, with shelves containing eight
thousand titles. Four computers were housed in carrels in the
back. Regarding her role, the coordinator said: "I try to get the
children to feel welcome in the resource center, to learn that it is
a place they can use. I try to get across that reading is more than
workbooks, that there is joy to be found in a good story."

At a small elementary school in Delaware, the Learning Resource Center is, quite literally, in the middle of the school.
When children step out of their classrooms, they see shelves
lined with books, and colorful banners saying "It's Fun to Read."
Rocking chairs invite "Grandteachers" to sit and read with students, and a "grandparent storytime" is scheduled every afternoon. There's a reading nook in one corner, on an elevated
platform with a ladder, where children curl up with a book. The
Center is used for group projects, too, with fourth-graders and
second-graders studying together. Students and teachers at the
school say the Resource Center is "everybody's classroom."

At one East Coast school, the librarian invites each student, on
his or her birthday, to choose a treasured book from the shelves.
The student's name is printed on a colorful bookplate inside the
front cover, and the book is then placed on display. The day we
were there, the librarian came to a first-grade classroom and

called the "birthday child" to her side. She held up the book, showed the class the dedicatory bookplate, and the child then told the class why she liked the book. The student then took the book home for the week, before returning it for the entire class to read.

The Basic School conveys a deep respect for the printed page to everyone in the school.

ELECTRONIC CLASSROOMS

Students in the Basic School also have access to the new technologies to enrich learning. Research reveals that students who use computers, for example, can become better readers and grasp abstract math concepts more thoroughly than do nonusers. Further, those who use word processing for writing become more sophisticated writers, outscoring other students in verbal creativity.[3]

In Santa Ana, California, students who studied science using English and bilingual videodiscs not only enjoyed the subject more, but scored higher on achievement tests than those who did not have such equipment.[4] In Indian River County, Florida, a new community-wide telecomputing network allows students to tap into educational software from their home, which has reduced television viewing among students by 40 percent.[5]

Seymour Papert, author of *The Children's Machine*, argues that: "Information technologies, from television to computers and all their combinations, open unprecedented opportunities for . . . improving the quality of the learning environment."[6]

Yet, despite its great potential, technology in most elementary school classrooms in this country is still shockingly deficient. Today, just 23 percent of the nation's elementary schools have CD-ROMS, only 21 percent have interactive videodisc players, and just 8 percent have a satellite dish for the retrieval of television signals (table 21).[7]

Especially troubling is the gap between the privileged and the disadvantaged. We were in affluent districts where students had the latest state-of-the-art hardware, while schools in our poorest communities had scarce books and a few broken-down projectors.

Frankly, it's shocking that almost every other enterprise in this country—from banks to airlines to hotels to places of commerce —has, quite literally, been transformed by technology. These companies simply could not carry on their work without it. But if all the technology were suddenly removed from *schools*, hardly anyone would notice. How can we be serious about educating our children for the next century when we've barely equipped them for *this* one?

In the Basic School, the goal is to make technology available to every student. While the pattern may vary from one school to the next, we recommend that by the year 2000 every classroom be electronically well equipped.

First, every classroom should have a television set and a videocassette player. In the 1950s, television was billed as an exciting teacher that would transform schools. The promise was to bring great teachers, electronically, to all students.[8] Unfortunately,

TABLE 21

U.S. ELEMENTARY SCHOOLS USING NEW TECHNOLOGIES

TYPE OF TECHNOLOGY	NUMBER OF SCHOOLS USING NEW TECHNOLOGY	PERCENTAGE OF TOTAL U.S. ELEMENTARY SCHOOLS
CD-ROM	11,794	23%
Interactive videodiscs	10,043	21
Satellite dish	4,269	8

SOURCE: Quality Education Data, Inc., *Technology in Public Schools 1993–94*, Denver, CO, 1994.

quality educational programming was in short supply and good programs, when they *were* aired, often were scheduled at times when students could not view them.

Today, VCRS make it possible for programs to be shown at convenient times, and it's estimated that over 75 percent of the nation's schools now have VCRS.[9] Further, the number of U.S. schools with cable television has risen nearly ten-fold in just three years— from a little over six thousand to more than sixty thousand.[10] Roughly 12 percent of schools now regularly use videodiscs, which bridge television and computers.[11]

The first step, then, is to provide a television set that can bring live or recorded programs to all students.

Second, all Basic School classrooms should have at least one computer for every five students, with a capacity for CD-*interactive discs.* The computer is, without question, the most popular and most versatile new resource. And more privileged students even have computer encyclopedias at home, with access to such services as *America Online*, which has "The Academic Assistance Center" to help students locate information on specific subjects. This service even includes a "Teacher Pager," which puts the student in direct contact with a teacher who comes "on line" to help with homework.[12]

Almost every school has at least a few computers. But unfortunately, computers are not conveniently available to *all* students, nor are they connected to the network beyond the school. Further, while 70 percent of the nation's elementary schools have a computer laboratory, less than 20 percent have several computers in each classroom within easy reach of students. Forty-two percent of the teachers in our survey reported that there is one computer in every classroom (table 22).

In the Basic School, we recommend that, as a minimum, one computer be made available for every five students in each class. Further, each teacher should have a computer for record-keeping, to prepare lesson plans, and to communicate with colleagues, with students, and even with parents.

Third, and perhaps the most essential, a telephone in each classroom is required. Why telephones? Today, only 12 percent of the nation's classrooms have telephones.[13] Yet, without a telephone or telephone line, there is simply no way for either the teacher or the students to have access to the new electronic highway—connecting into networks such as the Internet, which have almost limitless sources of knowledge.[14]

Telephones also open up communications between the teachers and parents. The Monforton School in Bozeman, Montana, for example, has a telephone in every classroom, and teachers use it

TABLE 22

WHICH OF THESE STATEMENTS BEST DESCRIBE ACCESS TO
SCHOOL COMPUTERS FOR YOUR STUDENTS?

	PERCENTAGE OF TEACHERS AGREEING
There is a computer lab in the school.	70%
There is one computer in your classroom.	42
There are several computers in your classroom.	19
There are a few computers which students can use.	15
Students do not have access to computers in the school.	5
There are no computers.	1

SOURCE: The Carnegie Foundation for the Advancement of Teaching and the George
H. Gallup International Institute, The International Schooling Project, 1994
(United States); each item is considered a separate question.

to reach out to parents. At a school in Fort Wayne, Indiana, teachers regularly put special assignments on telephone recorders. At the Hefferan Elementary School in Chicago, the staff believes that placing a telephone in each classroom—which enabled teachers to call parents on the spot—changed the entire climate of the school.

When it comes to technology, most schools have a long way to go.

As a first step, *planning* for technology can and should begin. And we urge that every Basic School develop its own Technology Master Plan, recognizing that the timetable will vary from school to school.

John See, an official with the Minnesota Department of Education, recommends that all technology plans have these common elements: Begin by asking *why* a particular technology is needed. Be open to *all kinds* of technology, not just computers. Always consider how technology can be *integrated* into the curriculum. Finally, include *staff development* in the plan.

Technology, no matter how sophisticated, will not work well in schools if teachers are intimidated by it or feel insecure. Yet nearly two-thirds of the nation's elementary teachers do *not* feel confident with computer technology, according to a national survey.[15] It's not that teachers are against technology. Rather, the real barrier, beyond the lack of up-to-date equipment, is insufficient teacher training and support. One elementary school teacher commented: "We have just spent thousands of dollars on new computers for each classroom and yet no one has taken five minutes to prepare us for what's been called the 'technology revolution.'"

We recommend, therefore, that in the Basic School no equipment be purchased and installed without involving teachers actively in the plan and providing adequate time for inservice training.

At David Cox Road Elementary School in Charlotte, North Carolina, technology has become a rich resource for learning, with teachers and students actively involved. Every classroom has a television monitor, a VCR, and computers, all interconnected. For special all-school presentations, if there is insufficient room in the auditorium, students can watch from their classrooms on closed-circuit TV. Within a David Cox classroom, a teacher can also engage eight or ten children with a computer-based lesson while working intensively with a group of students at another workstation. A video camera also is available. One student took the camera with her on a visit to her grandmother near Niagara Falls. With the help of an uncle, she selected special sights, wrote a script, and shot and narrated a video for her classmates back home, who, with technology, also took a trip to Niagara Falls.

When all is said and done, though, the most essential resource for learning in the Basic School is still the *teacher*. Television can take students to the moon and videotapes transport them to the bottom of the sea. Calculators can solve problems faster than the human brain. Computers can instantly retrieve millions of information bits and connect teachers and students to classrooms all around the world. Word processors can help children write and edit.

But there are times when the switches should be turned off. Technology cannot make value judgments. It cannot make students wise or able to distinguish the beautiful from the vulgar. For this we need *teachers*, not computers.

NEIGHBORHOODS FOR LEARNING

Finally, resources for learning in the Basic School extend beyond the classroom, and beyond the school itself. Whether in a calm farm village or a fast-paced urban community, children should view the entire neighborhood as an exciting place for learning.

A first-grade teacher at one urban school we visited plotted a large map of the two-block-long commercial street next to the school. It was a place most of the children passed through each morning. The teacher walked along the streets with her students and constructed a map of the territory, locating places they had seen. Every child took one section of the district, working hard to fill in accurately the details—putting everything to scale. Locations for learning were spotted, and then visited. When completed, the map was mounted on the wall. The neighborhood, for these students, became a classroom.

Author David McCullough recalls how, when he was growing up, the city of Pittsburgh became, for him, a classroom. "For along with the schools, besides all the programs in art and music, went the Carnegie Library, the Carnegie Museums, and Carnegie Music Hall, all in one great complex in the Oakland section of town. . . . I can hardly overstress the importance of this—that art, science, music, literature, history, the world of books, were joined, all together. . . . There were school trips to the Carnegie Museum of Natural History, free Saturday morning art classes at the Carnegie Museum of Art."[16]

San Francisco's Exploratorium is a wonderfully creative place for learning, as is the Children's Museum in Boston.[17] And just a few miles east of downtown Cleveland, in the University Circle, is the Cleveland Children's Museum, which becomes a classroom for thousands of students every year. One exhibit is an elaborate construction of small-scale bridges that can be raised, lowered, turned, and driven on. A waterway, complete with water currents and curving land masses, allows small-scale boats to be launched.

Educators in north central Ohio, who didn't have easy access to the Cleveland Museum, created one of their own. Today, twenty thousand school children from thirty school districts visit the McKinley Museum of Science and Industry in Canton. A natural history section features dinosaur bones, including a life-sized dinosaur skull which children can literally climb into. Students study the ecosystem of a pond. A "space station" is filled with magnetics for experiments, encouraging children to be creative learners.

At Jackson Elementary School in Everett, Washington, nearby Pigeon Creek is a classroom to five hundred students, from kindergarten through the fifth grade. After discovering that the creek was devoid of life and full of sludge, teachers and students designed a science curriculum to bring it back to life. In the first-grade wing of the school, a tank is stocked with baby salmon, then monitored, with the students noting the changes that come with the life cycle of the fish. Second- and third-grade students learn more about environmental issues in nature—how water becomes polluted, why the fish can't survive without clean water. Fourth-graders make regular trips to the creek to monitor water quality.

Each year, all students stock Pigeon Creek by releasing salmon fingerlings into the water. And Jackson Elementary School sponsors, annually, a "Salmon Celebration." "It definitely builds a sense of community, and this project has a way of sticking with them," says project coordinator Brandon King. "It's *their* Pigeon Creek." Further, what started as a school science curriculum has grown into a community project. The city has installed a new storm drainage system. A board of directors includes members from the PTA as well as city government. "This is one of those things that is good for the student, good for the teacher, and good for the community," said Mr. King. "And it has definitely brought the school together."

As we enter the new information age, we cannot deny children the rich resources for learning that can so powerfully expand their knowledge, spark their creativity, and intellectually transport them to classrooms in their neighborhoods, around the world, and even to the galaxies beyond.

Services for Children

The Basic School is committed to serving the whole child, acknowledging that a student's physical, social, and emotional well-being also relates to learning. Beyond a solid academic program, the school provides basic health and counseling services for students, referrals for families, and a new calendar and clock, with after-school and summer enrichment programs for learning and creative play.

It was Friday afternoon, the end of a busy week. A group of tired teachers in a Midwest school gathered in the crowded lounge. The conversation soon turned to troubled children. One veteran teacher said: "Frankly, I've noticed in the last few years that children's lives are not running smoothly. More and more of my students are upset when they come to school in the morning. They are often hungry, or distressed because of what's going on at home. Some are abused. I know I'm supposed to teach math and get ready for the next state reading exam. But how can I neglect these children who are hurting?"

In the Basic School, the focus always is on learning. The commitment is to assure that every student *educationally* succeeds. But a child who is sick, tired, hungry, or abused will find it difficult, even perhaps impossible, to be a confident, self-directed learner. And responding to the physical and emotional needs of children is both the educational *and* ethical thing to do. A third-grade teacher made the point precisely: "I just don't see how children can concentrate on reading if they're hungry or have a stomach ache."

Since the beginning of this century, when school nurses in Boston, New York, and other cities valiantly led the battle against infectious diseases and poor sanitation, and when young girls, trained in school, became "health teachers" in their homes, it has been widely accepted that good health relates to learning—that the educational and physical needs of children simply cannot be divided.[1]

By the 1920s, health services were well established in the nation's public schools. In large urban districts, for example, physicians came right to school. And most older Americans can recall the full-time school nurse who routinely scheduled health checkups, with vision, hearing, and dental screenings, and who, in an office just down the hall, cared for children with headaches, upset stomachs, or cuts and scrapes.

Recently, however, school-based health services have become casualties of budget cuts,[2] and what's especially disturbing is that these cutbacks are occurring at the very time the physical needs of children have increased. Consider, for example, that more than half the teachers we surveyed said that "undernourishment" is a problem at their school. Sixty-seven percent cited "poor health" as a problem.[3] A third-grade teacher in a midsized city observed: "Every year there seem to be more physical problems at our school that interfere with learning. I know that children who don't eat well or don't get rest can't do well in school. Yet that's exactly what I'm seeing more and more."

Emotional distress, even clinical depression, also is a growing problem among elementary school children, according to the National Association of School Nurses.[4] One Maryland teacher told us: "Sometimes I wish I were trained as a counselor as much as a teacher. I have so many students who aren't doing well in class because they are preoccupied with family problems in their lives." A veteran third-grade teacher told us: "I remember when we were expected just to educate the students. But now we're being asked to do everything for children. The schools are hopelessly overloaded."

To complicate the problem, nearly 90 percent of the parents we surveyed agreed that "families are not taking enough responsibility for the welfare of their children." Further, ninety-eight percent of the teachers said that "people are expecting schools to do too much" in response to social and emotional needs that once were considered to be the responsibility of the family (table 23).

Clearly, schools are caught in a dilemma. On the one hand, they encounter, daily, children who have physical and emotional needs that cannot be ignored. On the other hand, schools are *educational* institutions. They cannot and should not become "social service centers," act as surrogate parents, or seek to solve every family problem.

We propose, for the Basic School, a middle ground.

TABLE 23

ATTITUDES REGARDING THE EXPANDING ROLE OF SCHOOLS

	PERCENTAGE AGREEING	
	TEACHERS	PARENTS
People these days are expecting schools to do too much.	98%	75%
Over the past ten years, schools have taken more responsibility for children's needs.	98	62
Families are not taking enough responsibility for the welfare of their children.	96	89
In the future, schools should take more responsibility for the needs of children.	10	32

SOURCE: The Carnegie Foundation for the Advancement of Teaching and the George H. Gallup International Institute, The International Schooling Project, 1994 (United States).

While committed, first, to the academic achievement of each student, the focus of the Basic School still is on the whole child. Basic support services are provided by the school to meet the routine health and counsêling needs of children, with the recognition that such support, which is so essential to the *educational* mission of the institution, will vary from one school to the next.

In addition, the school provides a referral service, building a partnership with other community service agencies to respond to family needs that are more acute. And through optional after-school and summer enrichment programs, the Basic School ensures that the educational and social needs of children are met continuously throughout the year.

BASIC HEALTH SERVICE

Meeting the physical needs of students is, we discovered, a policy that has wide support. According to a national survey, almost 80 percent of the American people believe that providing health services in the school is "very important."[5] And most schools routinely evaluate the sight, hearing, and general health of students or require a physical when they enroll. However, our survey revealed that only about one-third of the nation's elementary schools have a nurse available daily. Forty-three percent have a nurse available at least once a week. Twelve percent have no school nurse at all (table 24).

School health service is as important now as it was at the turn of the century. Even generally healthy children have minor illnesses or cuts and bruises during the school day which if left unattended may lead to complications. In the case of contagious disease, the health of the whole school population is at stake. We recommend, therefore, that every Basic School offer basic health service, with at least a part-time registered nurse or nurse practitioner for routine services such as health screening, emergency first aid, health education, and disease control and prevention.[6]

One school we visited in the Southwest had a part-time school nurse paid by the county health department. Two parent volunteers, who had received health instruction, helped staff the clinic. The day we were there, the nurse was giving several children

TABLE 24

HOW OFTEN ARE THE SERVICES OF A NURSE
AVAILABLE FOR YOUR STUDENTS?

	PERCENTAGE AGREEING
Daily	34%
At least once a week	43
At least once a month	4
Several times a year	6
Not available	12

SOURCE: The Carnegie Foundation for the Advancement of Teaching, National Survey of Elementary School Principals, 1990.

their daily allergy shots. The parent aides helped four other children, one who had a stomach ache, another who had a fever, and two little girls on cots who said they "weren't feeling good." It was obvious that this nurse, working only along with parent volunteers, was making a big difference in the life of young students.

Other schools offer more extensive service. In New Haven, Connecticut, for example, 90 percent of the 469 students at the Katherine Brennan Elementary School participate in a comprehensive health program. The school clinic includes a nurse, a nurse practitioner, and a social worker. A pediatrician visits the school once a week, and four students from a nearby school of nursing help throughout the year.

At Porter Elementary School in Johnson County, Kentucky, a Family Resource Center features a full-time nurse practitioner who performs first aid, treats minor complaints, and completes physical examinations and TB screenings for all children. The center has achieved 100 percent immunizations for the school's 564 students. Before the center opened, children with minor complaints were often sent home. Now, with parental consent, the clinic can treat a child, administer prescribed medication, and send the child back to class. At Porter, the motto is: "Children learn better when children are in better shape to learn."

The Hamilton Elementary School in San Diego opened its family health center in 1991. Today it serves twelve hundred students. Located in an adjacent building on the school grounds, the Hamilton Center is staffed by a service coordinator, a nurse, and four employees of various city or county health and social service agencies. Doors are open from 7 A.M. to 6 P.M., to treat minor illnesses and complaints. Nurses also go to the homes of children to teach parents health and nutrition skills. Connie Busse, program director, says: "We're not a full health clinic. We don't want to be. We're trying to focus on prevention."[7]

The Basic School, while providing routine health care, focuses primarily on *prevention*. The health professionals in the school are considered *teachers*. The school nurse meets regularly with classes to talk about wellness and good food, the value of exercise, and the damage that drugs, alcohol, and tobacco can do. The goal is to help young students learn to respect and care for their own bodies. It's imperative to interrupt the cycle of ignorance about good health that diminishes, for so many children, the quality of their lives and also has such tragic consequences for the nation.

Helen Dugan, the school nurse at Center Elementary School in Kansas City, Missouri, is a gifted teacher who meets with all the students. She is enthusiastically welcomed into classrooms by colleagues. Offering a creative health curriculum that focuses on prevention, she teaches about dental health, drugs, and personal hygiene. She invigorates classrooms, often using a puppet stage in the doorway, while the children inside call out questions and the puppets respond. Ms. Dugan says, "Teaching children about their own bodies and giving them skills to help their families is a big step toward prevention."

BASIC COUNSELING SERVICE

It's obvious that children who are deeply troubled or emotionally distracted cannot concentrate successfully on academic tasks. To promote learning, a professional counseling program is a basic service in every Basic School. Mary Futrell, of George Washington University, observes that the relationship between a child's emotions and learning is a phenomenon every classroom teacher understands. "[J]ust as a child who is hungry cannot learn, so too a child who is wracked with anxiety or mired in depression or burdened with self-hatred cannot learn."[8]

Adults often forget what it's like to be little. According to an Iowa survey, children worry most about "a family member getting sick." The next highest worry was "doing well on tests." Nearly 70 percent said they also worry about "what parents think of their work" (table 25).[9]

And tragically, many children are coping with extremely debilitating problems, at a level that would test the most resilient adult. Schools—and communities—simply must do more to meet children's emotional needs, which can be shockingly acute.[10]

TABLE 25

WHAT THIRD-GRADE CHILDREN WORRY ABOUT

	PERCENTAGE AGREEING
A family member getting sick or hurt	77%
Doing well on tests	71
What parents think of their work	68
Drugs and alcohol	60
Safety of the neighborhood	55
Problems in the family	54
Children tattling on them	52
Being teased	47
Making good decisions	38
People getting too angry	34
Knowing what to do when they get angry	33

SOURCE: Jan Kuhl, "Report on Children's Needs Survey," administered by the Des Moines Elementary Counselors, Des Moines, Iowa; items selected from a survey of third-graders. "Percentage Agreeing" indicates the proportion of third-grade children agreeing with each item.

In his powerfully moving book, *Not All of Us Are Saints*, David Hilfiker, a medical doctor, tells about how the play of young children in the city reflects at a very early age the emotional crises in their lives. "When still very young, they play at being police officers, firefighters, doctors, and teachers," he writes. "But . . . at about six years of age, things begin to change. In their games the children now begin to play addict, pusher, and narcotics agent. They play drunk; they play out fights between men and women, between parent and child. . . . Hope has already been crushed."[11]

The sad truth is that in most elementary schools, the counseling service available to children is insufficient, or even nonexistent.

Today, only 31 percent of the nation's elementary schools have daily counseling service; 36 percent have such service at least once a week, according to the principals (table 26). And in elementary schools where counseling services do exist, the ratio averages one counselor for four hundred and fifty to five hundred students.[12] In some large urban schools, where the need is often greatest, one counselor may serve up to eight hundred pupils.[13]

A third-grade teacher in Kentucky talked poignantly about the pain she felt at seeing children's emotional turmoil, and then added: "Tight funding has left my school without a counselor, and teachers have to decide each day whether they are teachers *or* counselors." A second-grade teacher made a similar observation: "Some days it's hard for me to know if I'm here to teach or to give emotional support to children who are hurting."

In the Basic School, counseling is so intimately woven into the daily routine of school life that it is impossible to separate it from teaching. Every elementary school teacher is continuously engaged in giving guidance and support—with a reassuring smile, a gentle pat, or pausing to listen attentively to a troubled child. But such engagement, while essential, can be insufficient. We recommend, specifically, that each Basic School also have at least a part-time counselor, to whom teachers can make referrals, and, when necessary, such professional support should be expanded.

The Coventry Elementary School in Cleveland Heights, Ohio, has a full-time counselor. In addition to meeting the needs of individual students, Bruce Fink, the counselor, focuses on prevention. Working with one or two classes each day, he helps students make decisions or solve problems, and works with upper-

TABLE 26

TO WHAT EXTENT ARE COUNSELING SERVICES AVAILABLE FOR YOUR STUDENTS?

	COUNSELOR	PSYCHOLOGIST	SOCIAL WORKER
Daily	31%	8%	7%
At least once a week	36	47	31
At least once a month	3	13	6
Several times a year	3	17	17
Not available	28	16	40

SOURCE: The Carnegie Foundation for the Advancement of Teaching, National Survey of Elementary School Principals, 1990.

grade students on "healthy chemicals" and "unhealthy chemicals," integrating his instruction with the health curriculum units. The counselor introduces fifth-graders to the world of work, discussing such questions as, "How do you relate personal interests to vocational ones?"

In commenting on his experience, Mr. Fink said: "Guidance is usually seen as necessary in junior high and high school. But at the elementary level, we can help before problems become deeply entrenched. I was a counselor in the high school for nine years, the middle school for three. I have been here at Coventry Elementary for seven years, and this is the only place where I see real results."

We visited one elementary school where the full-time counselor meets regularly with teachers to talk about children with special needs, and also visits classrooms as a guest teacher. A colorful mailbox in the corridor just outside her office invites children to leave confidential notes or ask for an appointment. Teachers make referrals anytime. This counselor also hosts lunches each day in her office for four or five children who are referred by teachers. Students view these lunches as something special. Teachers told us that the counseling program improves the academic performance of students, as they become emotionally more secure.

In Des Moines, Iowa, a districtwide counseling program called "Smoother Sailing" has been introduced. With support from area businesses, school counselors from across the city were able to design their own curriculum handbook. Counselors were then assigned to schools, with a 250-to-1 student-counselor ratio. The program has paid off. Teachers see a difference. Des Moines schools report a decline in discipline and attendance problems, as well as improvement in academic test scores. "The turmoil in children's lives is smoothed out by Smoother Sailing," said Barbara Sloan, a Des Moines principal. "It's a fantastic addition to our schools."[14]

AFTERNOON AND SUMMER SERVICES

The Basic School also is responsive to the changing work and family schedule. In yesterday's agrarian society, when most families lived on farms, children hurried home each day to help with chores and stayed home in the summer to cultivate and harvest crops. School life and family life were inseparably related, with the school schedule reflecting the realities of home and work.

Today, the calendar and the clock which still regulate many schools are seriously out of step with the realities of modern family life.[15] Children have few chores to do. Most parents now work *away* from home. Every afternoon "latchkey kids" go home to an empty house,[16] and children everywhere are socially and educationally disengaged during the summer months.

As the gap between work and family life has widened, children have become increasingly more isolated from the adult world. They spend more and more time alone or with other children of similar age. According to a Carnegie Foundation survey, 30 percent of fifth-graders go home every afternoon to an empty house. Nearly two-thirds said they wish they had more things to do. And a quarter of fifth-graders say they are often lonely (table 27).

"Children have become increasingly isolated from the adult world, and plain loneliness leaves them with very little curiosity, very little interest in learning," one Missouri teacher said. A teacher in Massachusetts commented: "Many of my students just hang around at the end of every day. They ask what they can do to help me. Often there's no one at home, and they're afraid to go home or spend time on the streets." Another teacher said: "It is unacceptable to send children off in the afternoon and know that they are unattended, drifting in the street."

Responding to this challenge, the Basic School offers a voluntary before- and after-school enrichment program, as well as "extended year" programs in the summer. For families who are able to pay, a fee is charged. For parents classified as poor, such services should be subsidized by public or private funds. Further, afternoon and summer programs should be staffed with a second

TABLE 27

ISSUES OF CONCERN TO FIFTH-GRADERS

	PERCENTAGE AGREEING
When I come home from school, there is usually an adult there to meet me.	70%
I often wish I had more things to do.	62
I am often lonely.	24

SOURCE: The Carnegie Foundation for the Advancement of Teaching, Survey of Fifth- and Eighth-Graders, 1988.

team of teachers and counselors, city recreation leaders, or other volunteers, including retirees as well as college students.

Since 1990, the After-School Plus (A+) Program in Hawaii has created an afternoon enrichment program in every school in the state. The purpose: to develop a sense of *ohana*, the Hawaiian word for a "feeling of belonging." Participating children choose such activities as art, drama, and sports, or they do homework. The program, which operates from 2 P.M. to 5 P.M., is for students in kindergarten through sixth grade.[17]

In Murfreesboro, Tennessee, eight elementary schools remain open twelve hours a day, some beginning at 6 A.M. The extended day gives children more time to pursue music, art, drama, computers, and foreign language. Participating families pay a small fee for each child. Students from nearby Middle Tennessee State University work alongside volunteers to staff the program.

Basic Schools may also wish to offer an extended summer program as an option for families. An increasing number of school districts are switching to year-round plans to provide enrichment or remediation. Today, over two thousand public schools are extending their school year into the summer months, and over one million elementary children now go to school year-round.[18]

Buena Vista, Virginia, has operated what it calls a Four Seasons Calendar for the last twenty years, with an optional summer program for enrichment, outdoor classes, and skill reinforcement. School superintendent James Bradford estimates the district saves $100,000 a year on retention costs as students take more time but then earn their promotion to the next grade. "Given more time, kids learn more," said Mr. Bradford. "That's the bottom line."

Saturday programs can enrich learning, too. The Saturday Science Academy in Atlanta, for example, sponsored by Clark Atlanta University, is one of the oldest programs in the country. It offers 150 students in third through eighth grades enrichment programs in math, science, writing, and public speaking.

Dade County in Florida uses Saturday Academies to concentrate on reading and math, which are incorporated in programs with such titles as "Architectural Math," "Earth Science Investigations for Young Scientists," and "Motion Unlimited: An Experience with Dance." And at Jackson-Keller in San Antonio, Texas, with its high rate of student turnover, Saturday is actually a time for students *and* parents to attend school together.

Extending the school calendar and clock pays off.[19] Researchers at The Johns Hopkins University report that giving students extra time before and after school to focus on reading and math improves achievement levels.[20] Further, children who consistently attend summer school do more reading than those of similar income levels who do not attend.[21] Yale University professor Edward Zigler observes that extending school services increases a child's ability to succeed academically and also puts school buildings to fuller use. "We've got well over a trillion dollars invested in these schools," notes Zigler. "Why don't we use them more fully?"[22]

NETWORKS FOR CHILDREN

Many schools encounter crises that they are simply not equipped to handle—home violence, child abuse, even homelessness. During one school visit, a mother showed up in a third-grade classroom at eight o'clock Monday morning. She told the teacher that the father had been violent over the weekend and "I have no place else to go."

No arbitrary line can be drawn between the school and life outside. Every Basic School should take the lead in organizing a *referral service*—a community safety net for children that links students and their families to support agencies in the region—to clinics, family support and counseling centers, and religious institutions.[23] "All of our children are growing up in a world at risk, and we as adults have a collective obligation to do something about it," notes Allan Shedlin, Jr., executive director of the Elementary School Center.[24]

James P. Comer, Yale University child psychiatrist, has pioneered collaboration among professionals, to support children. There are now more than two hundred "Comer Schools" in nineteen states and the District of Columbia. With the Comer Model, a professional team provides social and emotional intervention for young children, combining classroom teachers and outside professionals—mental health workers and social workers. The team actively involves parents, too.

Perhaps the time has come to organize, in every community, not just a *school* board, but a *children's* board. The goal would be to integrate children's services and build, in every community, a friendly, supportive environment for children.

The Charlotte-Mecklenburg Board of Education in North Carolina decided, several years ago, to focus not just on schools, but on *children*. A coordination of services was required. Mayor Richard Vinroot set the tone when he said: "Education involves more than what happens between 9:00 A.M. and 3:00 P.M. five days a week." In response, the school board organized a Children's Services Network. The network, which brings together all of the community agencies concerned with children, coordinates the services, increases support, and prepares a report card on progress.[25] This could be a model for other communities.

The Beverly School District in Massachusetts has a board of counselors, school nurses, and community medical care providers to assist teachers with health education in the classroom. In New Haven, Connecticut, a health board composed of teachers, students, and parents meets monthly to make suggestions about how to improve its school clinic. In some communities, the school building itself may be used by several different agencies to bring services to children—and families.

In Palm Beach County, Florida, local officials created a special taxing district to support children's programs, administered by an independent government agency called Children's Services

Council. After a countywide survey, the ten-member council identified sixteen priorities—from reducing school dropouts to improving child care. Nearly sixty children's projects have been launched, including infant nurseries, intervention programs for kids with special needs, and parent support groups. On the West Coast, a recent referendum in Seattle requires that a portion of tax money be used to increase services in the elementary school.

Children *can* become a community priority.

In our hard-edged, competitive world, a community-wide commitment to help children may seem quixotic. Not only has the sense of neighborhood faded, but the very notion of community seems strikingly inapplicable to contemporary life. Absent larger loyalties, we are settling for little loyalties that diminish our national unity and widen the social separations. There's a growing pessimism in this country, a feeling that the social pathologies we now confront may be just too deep to be remedied.

But good will runs deep in America. Throughout our history, citizens have shown their capacity to come together and organize energetically in times of crisis. We have dedicated ourselves to great causes, responding in times of need with vigor and an outpouring of concern. We are confident that with the right blend of commitment and imagination, communities in this nation can come together, once again, this time on behalf of children.[26]

A COMMITMENT TO CHARACTER

The Core Virtues

> *The Basic School is concerned with the ethical and moral dimensions of a child's life. The goal is to assure that all students, on leaving school, will have developed a keen sense of personal and civic responsibility. Seven core virtues, such as respect, compassion, and perseverance, are emphasized to guide the Basic School as it promotes excellence in living, as well as learning.*

We have considered, thus far, three priorities for the Basic School: first, bringing *people* together, to build *community*; second, bringing the *curriculum* together, to achieve *coherence*; third, bringing *resources* together, to enrich *climate*. The fourth priority, *A Commitment to Character*, raises the issue of how everything we have talked about for the Basic School affects the lives of children. Will what students learn touch their deeper selves and help them not only become knowledgeable, but socially and ethically responsible as well?

Once, the focus of education was on body, mind, *and* spirit. Values, taught at home, and during worship, were reinforced at school. In 1837, Horace Mann, the father of the common school, insisted that public schools should help students develop both

173

reason *and* conscience.[1] "The highest and noblest office of education . . . ," Mann wrote, "pertains to our moral nature." The common school, according to Mann, should teach virtue before knowledge, for although the latter should not be ignored, knowledge without virtue poses its own dangers.[2]

Today, not only has the commitment to teach "virtue before knowledge" dramatically declined, but educators are often made to feel uncomfortable even talking about such matters. It's all right these days to speak of *academic* standards, but if the talk turns to *ethical* standards an awkward silence seems to settle in. What's especially disturbing is the way this void is often filled for children by media messages that portray, even glorify, evil actions, leading to negative behavior and, in the extreme, to what columnist William Raspberry chillingly describes as a "consciencelessness" among many children.[3]

It's true that most elementary school students live positive, responsible lives and during school visits we were reassured, often inspired, by the way young children demonstrate kindness to others—living by the rules, trying to make sense of the moral ambiguities that surround them.[4]

Still, teachers frequently spoke about what they believe to be a decline in ethical standards among children that is often reflected, they said, on the playground and even in the classroom. In one fourth-grade class a student couldn't find his scarf and suspected it had been stolen. After searching for the object, the teacher discussed the problem with the class. Getting only a grudging response, she asked how many thought it was all right to steal. Nearly 80 percent said "yes," provided, they all agreed, "you don't get caught."

TABLE 28

WHICH OF THESE ARE SERIOUS PROBLEMS IN YOUR SCHOOL:
CHEATING, STEALING, AND STUDENTS MAKING NOISE AND
DISRUPTING CLASS?

(PERCENTAGE OF STUDENTS AGREEING)

	CHEATING	STEALING	STUDENTS MAKING NOISE AND DISRUPTING CLASS
Chile	66%	51%	88%
Mexico	53	52	75
Israel	49	45	72
Zimbabwe	48	61	49
Russia	47	59	55
Turkey	47	48	73
UNITED STATES	45	38	67
Germany	42	34	59
Great Britain	36	39	59
China	22	24	21
Italy	16	22	71
Japan	12	11	15

SOURCE: The Carnegie Foundation for the Advancement of Teaching and the George
H. Gallup International Institute, The International Schooling Project, 1994.

Students, themselves, also report negative conduct in their schools. In our survey of nine- to eleven-year-olds in this country, 45 percent said "cheating" is a serious problem. Thirty-eight percent identified "stealing" as a serious problem. Sixty-seven percent said "students often making noise and disrupting class" is a serious problem at their school (table 28). One teacher summarized the situation this way: "I feel what I see these days is the 'Okay Generation.' No matter what the circumstances, everything will be 'okay.' Consequences seem to have no meaning for so many children."

The harsh truth is that knowledge unguided by an ethical compass is potentially more dangerous than ignorance itself. A century after Horace Mann, the world learned what can happen ultimately when knowledge is devoid of virtue. George Steiner, in reflecting on the Holocaust, vividly describes it. "We know now," he writes, "that a man can read Goethe or Rilke in the evening, that he can play Bach and Schubert, and go to his day's work at Auschwitz in the morning." What grows up inside literate civilization, Steiner asks, that prepares "it for the release of barbarism?"[5]

What grows up, of course, is information without knowledge, knowledge without wisdom, competence without conscience.

PLACES TO BUILD CHARACTER

The conclusion is clear: The Basic School, while helping students become literate and well informed, also has a duty, along with parents and religious institutions, to help children develop the capacity to live responsibly and judge wisely in matters of life and conduct. But where do we begin? How do we help students develop what Horace Mann called reason *and* conscience? Whose responsibility is it anyway?

First, the family. Parents, without question, are primarily responsible for a child's ethical instruction. There can be no substitute for a mother and father who, from the very first, provide loving guidance and define for the child—both by what they say and how they live—standards of good conduct. This is, in fact, an obligation most parents understand. Seventy percent of the U.S.

TABLE 29

WHICH OF THESE DO YOU THINK HAS PRIMARY RESPONSIBILITY
FOR DEVELOPING VALUES IN CHILDREN: MOSTLY THE FAMILY,
MOSTLY THE SCHOOL, OR SHARED BY FAMILY AND SCHOOL?
(PERCENTAGE OF PARENTS AGREEING)

	MOSTLY THE FAMILY	MOSTLY THE SCHOOL	SHARED BY FAMILY AND SCHOOL
UNITED STATES	70%	1%	29%
Germany	58	2	40
Mexico	50	0	50
Italy	47	0	53
Russia	46	2	52
Chile	44	1	55
Great Britain	44	1	56
Japan	43	1	56
Zimbabwe	25	3	72
Turkey	23	5	72
Israel	22	1	76
China	7	9	84

SOURCE: The Carnegie Foundation for the Advancement of Teaching and the George
H. Gallup International Institute, The International Schooling Project, 1994.

parents we surveyed agree that the family has the *primary* responsibility "for developing values in children."

Other countries vary greatly in their views regarding the role of parents, a fact that reflects deep differences among cultures. In China, for example, only 7 percent of the parents assigned the responsibility for developing children's values to the family. No country, however, considered it to be mostly the responsibility of the school (table 29).

When it comes to character building, family is the key. Parents are not just the first teachers, as important as that is. They are the first *models*. There is simply no substitute for a mother and father who form a loving and supportive circle around the child, presenting, by direct instruction and example, the precepts of good living, the virtues of a well-directed life.

Author and commentator Cheri Fuller reminds us that the child may have many teachers along the way, but parents are the primary instructors and guides. And surely one of our most urgent obligations, as a society and as educators, is to lend support to parents, who must assume the major responsibility for teaching values to the coming generation.

Second, places of worship. Traditionally, religious institutions have played a consequential role in the spiritual guidance of children, setting a high moral standard, and should be strong *teachers* of virtue, too. Churches and mosques and synagogues respond, according to their own tenets, to the most profound questions children ask. Robert Coles, Harvard University psychiatrist, writes that all children have an innate interest in "the ultimate meaning of life, in the sacred side of things," and ask questions about the mystery of creation and about how religious experience relates to life.[6]

Private schools may address such questions. Public schools, while restricted by the Constitution from religious instruction can, however, adopt "released-time" arrangements, making it possible for students to leave school, with parent consent, for religious training.[7] Released time has, in fact, been part of the public school system since 1914, and today, an estimated four hundred thousand students participate nationwide in released time. School policies in Fort Wayne, Salt Lake City, and Minneapolis, for example, grant public school students up to two or three hours every week to attend instructional programs sponsored by religious institutions.[8]

Each Basic School must decide for itself whether a released-time program is consistent with community expectations.

Finally, the schools. Teaching virtues cannot be left entirely to the home and religious institutions. After all, children spend about 180 days a year in school. Formal education is one of the most powerful forces in their lives. Public schools also must assume responsibility for character building.

High academic standards and high ethical standards are inseparably connected. According to a national poll, nearly 90 percent of the American people believe that emphasizing "habits of discipline" in the school would make "a great deal of difference" in student achievement.[9] Several years ago, the U.S. Department of Education wanted to find out why a group of award-winning schools was so successful. The study concluded that while "academics" remained the central mission, these effective schools were equally concerned about "good character."[10]

A good school is, in fact, always teaching values. A commitment to education rather than ignorance is a value. Working hard, getting to school on time, completing assignments, and respecting teachers are all values that go to the very heart of education.

Author William Kilpatrick powerfully makes this point: "If students . . . don't learn habits of courage and justice, curriculums designed to improve their self-esteem won't stop the epidemic of extortion, bullying, and violence. . . . Even academic reform depends on putting character first. Children need courage to tackle difficult assignments. They need self-discipline if they are going to devote their time to homework rather than television. . . . If they don't acquire intellectual virtues such as commitment to learning, objectivity, respect for the truth, and humility in the face of facts, then critical-thinking strategies will only amount to one more gimmick in the curriculum."[11]

REACHING CONSENSUS

Almost everyone seems to acknowledge the importance of character building. And for the Basic School to be fully successful, virtues must be consciously affirmed, an intentional part of the school program. The real problem is deciding which virtues should be taught. There is a widespread feeling that, with all of the diversity in America today, no consensus can be reached. The most frequently asked question is, "Whose values?"

The "values debate" often focuses almost exclusively on the *contested* issues, those relating to religion, politics, sexuality, and life styles where, because of conscience or personal preference, differences are deep-rooted and emotions run high. Yet, without diminishing these crucial matters, we conclude that there is, in fact, a core of *consensus virtues* on which practically everyone might agree.[12] It is here where our search for common ground should focus. And perhaps if the *consensus virtues* would be more forthrightly affirmed and taught each day, our ability to resolve conflicts in *contested* areas also might improve.

The prospects for such a possibility seem to be emerging. E. D. Hirsch, Jr., author of *Cultural Literacy*, writes about consensus values.[13] Thomas Shannon, executive director of the National School Boards Association, said recently there are "a vast number of [values] on which we can agree."[14] Paul Houston, executive director of the American Association of School Administrators, suggests: "There's a lot of consensus on which values are going to be taught."[15]

Recently a national coalition of more than twenty organizations, ranging from the Association for Supervision and Curriculum Development to McDonnell Douglas Corp., formed a Character Education Partnership dedicated, according to its mission statement, to "developing civic virtue and moral character in our youth for a more compassionate and responsible society."[16]

There is, in short, a growing sense of urgency in this country that all of us should affirm for our children a core of virtues to enrich their learning and guide their lives. James Q. Wilson, in his insightful book *The Moral Sense*, says that such universally held values and beliefs would include sympathy, fairness, self-control, and duty. William J. Bennett, in his best-selling anthology, *The Book of Virtues*, presents ten "time-honored understandings"—self-discipline, compassion, responsibility, friendship, work, courage, perseverance, honesty, loyalty, and faith.[17]

School districts, too, have to become more active in this essential dimension of education. Five years ago, The Allen Traditional Academy Elementary School, in Dayton, Ohio, began emphasizing such values as responsibility and respect for others. At that time, it placed twenty-eighth among the city's thirty-three elementary schools in test scores. Since it began to openly build core virtues into the daily life of students, the school has climbed to fifth place academically among the city's schools.[18] Last fall,

all forty-seven public schools in Dayton acknowledged the importance of helping students build character. Flyers are sent to parents suggesting learning activities that might illustrate a certain trait. Businesses, the religious community, the public library, and community organizations help reinforce the virtues.[19]

St. Louis, Missouri, created a character program with community participation.[20] Consensus was reached that honesty, responsibility, cooperation, and commitment should be taught. Some twenty-four school districts within St. Louis—344 schools serving about 200,000 students—are involved. Each school decides how these character traits are taught, through word and action. Some have "friendship activities" and carefully guided discussions about "getting along with others," and about heroes in history whose lives have made a difference.[21] Over forty local foundations, businesses, and individuals formed partnerships to provide funds for resources, publicity, and parent and teacher training.

Last year, in Milford, Delaware, Kae E. Keister, principal of Banneker Elementary School, organized a "values committee" composed of parents, teachers, school board members, and nine clergy from various faiths to see what agreement could be reached on "time-honored understandings." The goal, according to the local school board, was to strengthen the role of parents and religious institutions, recognizing that the school staff—principal, teachers, custodians, secretaries, bus drivers—do teach values, implicitly, as they serve as role models for children.[22]

After lively conversations and public hearings, this citizen's group unanimously affirmed six values that, they concluded, were appropriate for all students. These were: compassion, integrity, perseverance, respect, responsibility, and self-control.

Dr. Keister, in describing the process, told us: "Working with the values committee was most rewarding. We all came from many backgrounds, and to agree on core values was both exciting and affirming. Most exciting has been the way these values can be drawn into the life of the school, both in the general climate and in the curriculum. We are making a difference in the lives of children."

Banneker School reached consensus. Others can, too.

BASIC VIRTUES

Every Basic School should affirm its own *commitment to character*, seeking to define, through community-wide consultation, those virtues most appropriate for students as well as others at their school. The list will surely vary from one school to the next. But, as a starting point, we suggest the following seven virtues for the Basic School, which draw heavily on the Banneker School experience:

- *Honesty*. Each person carries out his or her responsibilities carefully and with integrity, never claiming credit for someone else's work and being willing to acknowledge wrongdoing. Students and staff share their ideas openly, in a climate of trust, with confidence that what is written and spoken is honestly expressed and that all people are trustworthy.

- *Respect*. Each person responds sensitively to the ideas and needs of others without dismissing or degrading them. Differences among people are celebrated, and all members of the community are able to accept both praise and constructive suggestions from others. While affirming individual freedom, the rights of the group are also fully honored.

· *Responsibility*. Each person has a sense of duty to fulfill willingly the tasks he or she has accepted or has been assigned. All work is conscientiously performed. Members of the community feel comfortable asking for help and agree that they must be held accountable for their behavior.

· *Compassion*. Each person is considerate and caring. There is a recognition that everyone, from time to time, feels hurt, confused, angry, or sad. Instead of ignoring such conditions, people reach out to one another. In the case of conflict, members of the community seek reconciliation and try to understand each other, even forgive.

· *Self-discipline*. Each person agrees to live within limits, not only the ones mutually agreed upon, but, above all, those established personally. Self-discipline is exercised in relationships with others, especially in the way people speak to one another. Self-discipline also applies to the use of time. At the simplest level, self-control reflects habits of good living.

· *Perseverance*. Each person is diligent, with the inner strength and determination to pursue well-defined goals. It *does* matter that a task be completed once begun, and to persevere not only teaches discipline, but brings rewards as well. Each person pushes hard to complete assignments, and all members of the community willingly support others in their work.

· *Giving.* Each person discovers that one of life's greatest satisfactions comes from giving to others, and recognizes that talents should be shared, through service. Rather than waiting to be asked, members of the community look for opportunities to respond positively to the needs of others, without expectation of reward.

At the end of the Basic School, students will have started to think about life's most important questions. They will have discovered that what they learn in school really does make a difference in their lives, that it will touch their deeper selves and help them become more knowledgeable, responsible human beings.

Living with Purpose

> *The core virtues of the Basic School are taught both by word and deed. Through the curriculum, through school climate, and through service, students are encouraged to apply the lessons of the classroom to the world around them.*

We come, finally, to the question: "How can virtues be taught in public schools?" Defining virtues is one thing, but what does this mean in actual school practice? Different educational approaches have been tried. Some schools identify character as a subject to be taught. Others give students case studies to work through and solve. We conclude that character building relates to the entire school experience and can be taught through the curriculum, through school climate, and through service.

CHARACTER THROUGH CURRICULUM

First, in the Basic School, teaching virtues is included in what is taught, but not necessarily as a separate course on "character" education or as an exercise in "values clarification." Rather, what we have in mind is discovering lessons in virtue across the whole curriculum. In Hopewell, Virginia, students study heroes and heroines in history who, by their lives, exemplify virtue. They learn from Cochise about truth and trust; from Jane Addams, friendship; from Frederick Douglass, freedom. And Thomas Edison's biography offers a wonderful example of creativity and persistence.[1]

Basic School students read great literature and talk about stories that reveal larger truths. They memorize poems that inspire them to be honest, to persevere, and to be compassionate. *The Little Match Girl*, by Hans Christian Andersen, illustrates the need for compassion. *A Tale of Three Wishes*, by Isaac Bashevis Singer, reveals how wishes must be earned. *The Emperor and the Kite*, by Jane Yolen, is a tale of courage and loyalty set in ancient China. Some schools have used *The Little Engine That Could* to stress persistence and hard work. "Stories help to make sense of our lives," notes author William Kilpatrick.[2]

For young children even simple songs and verses are lessons in character. At the Waldorf School in Princeton, New Jersey, students start each day reciting verses aimed at instilling strength and helping students develop a sense of who they are. One verse recited by a second-grader goes like this:

> Straight as a spear we stand,
> Strength fills our legs and arms,
> Warmth in our hearts,
> And love for our work in the world.

Rich lessons in character can be discovered within the Core Commonalities of the Basic School. In the Life Cycle, for example, children study health, physical education, and how the body functions. But the deeper lesson is that life is sacred, that we all must be respectful of one another. In the Use of Symbols, they learn that honesty is the key to thoughtful discourse. Exploring a Sense of Time and Space, they study heroes of the past. In learning about the Response to the Aesthetic, children are inspired by the beauty in life.

Students, during the years of the Basic School, learn discipline and persistence in the methods of science by studying Connections to Nature. In exploring Membership in Groups, students begin to understand personal rights and responsibilities. In considering Producing and Consuming, children learn the value of hard work and the virtue of honesty. And all of these come together as students reflect on Living with Purpose, learning that, to be fully human, one must serve.

In the Basic School, the curriculum builds character.

CHARACTER THROUGH CLIMATE

A school's greatest impact occurs not in the formal lessons taught, but in people's lives—what's been called "the hidden curriculum." The challenge of the Basic School is to create a climate in which virtues are learned by example.

At Captain Elementary School in St. Louis, teachers, students, and parents enter into a "caring contract" that establishes clear, mutual expectations for good conduct by everyone. As a result, students become more disciplined and more inclined to be helpful. Orchard School in Ridgewood, New Jersey, ends each day with children publicly thanking fellow students as well as teachers for help they've received that day. Children also can be rewarded for their deeds. The elementary school in North Webster, Indiana, selects from among its students the "Citizen of the Week."

Etna Road Elementary School in Whitehall, Ohio, announces a character "Word of the Week." Recently, "respect" was highlighted. Students learned about "respect for self" and "respect for others and their property" as the new school year opened. Each day principal James Rodenmayer broadcasts a friendly reminder of the "Word of the Week," with comments about why it is so important.

One afternoon we talked with a fifth-grade teacher in a large urban school. She commented on the pressures children face and her own personal commitment to character building. She described the challenge this way: "I look around at the world my students are growing up in, the violence on the streets and on TV, and ask, 'What can I do?' I decided that I can teach them to be courteous in my class, to respect one another, to be honest with one another and me, to learn to care about each other, and respect what belongs to each other. I can refuse to have foul language in my presence, to teach them to say 'thank you' and 'excuse me.'"

"It didn't take long," she said. "When swear words slipped out, students were catching themselves, saying 'I'm sorry,' or 'excuse me.' Property that had been taken was 'mysteriously' found. The classroom climate changed. Student performance improved. I felt I was teaching them not only how to learn, but how to live."

Character was being built through the climate of the classroom.

CHARACTER THROUGH SERVICE

Ultimately, virtues take on meaning when they are lived. "We become just by doing just acts, temperate by doing temperate acts, brave by doing brave acts," Aristotle observed.[3] A sense of service is expected among adults, but a commitment to civic duty doesn't just emerge. It begins early, and if we want good citizenship among older people, it surely must become a part of children's lives.

In his recent book *Greater Expectations*, William Damon elegantly states the challenge: "Even if our children were being raised to become the best informed, most artistic, and healthiest children that the world has ever seen, it would all come to nothing unless they found some things beyond themselves. . . . Even if children took their math homework and piano lessons far more seriously than they do now, they would still need to develop a sense of social responsibility. They would still need to care for other people, to work for the good of others. . . . Otherwise they could not live together in a decent society, nor pass along what is left of the culture to their own children."[4]

We recommend, therefore, that every student in the Basic School learn to serve, with chores at home and school, with work on projects at the church, mosque, or synagogue, giving a helping hand to older people, to children at a day-care center and, of course, to other students in the school.[5]

"Service is a life-long commitment" is the mission statement at the Washington Elementary School in Mount Vernon, Washington. Service is woven into every aspect of the program. In grades one through three, students learn to help another person, to listen carefully to others, to give encouragement to others, and to answer questions thoughtfully and with respect. In fourth grade, all students tutor a younger child. In grade five, each student has a service project outside the school, as a library helper or safety patrol leader, for example.

Every year, each classroom at Washington School plans its own service project. One year kindergartners organized a "Trash Patrol." First-graders had a "Japanese Friendship Exchange." Second-graders made a quilt for a homeless shelter. Third-graders planted flowers for a school beautification project. Fourth-graders organized a "senior citizen" partnership. Fifth-graders started a bird sanctuary on the school grounds, for beauty as well as conservation.[6] At Washington Elementary School, virtues are *lived*.

Imagine what would happen if families, and places of worship, and schools—joined by television writers and radio talk show hosts, recording artists, athletes, movie stars, business executives, and politicians—all would agree to teach children, by both word and example, *honesty*, *respect*, *responsibility*, *compassion*, *self-discipline*, *perseverance*, and *giving*. What if all of the adults, who seem so upset about the troubled lives of children, would indeed create a climate in which these core virtues would become, for all of us, a way of life?

When all is said and done, the Basic School is a *community*, with a coherent curriculum, a climate for learning, and a commitment to character, one that helps students develop the capacity to judge wisely and act responsibly in matters of life and conduct. The goal is not only to prepare students for careers, but also to enable them to live with dignity and purpose; not only to give knowledge to the student, but also to channel knowledge to humane ends.

In the end, students in the Basic School will have their own sense of the sacredness of life, understanding, at a basic level, the miracle of their own bodies and the importance of being respectful of life in all its forms. They will know that we all use symbols to relate to one another, which is a miracle in itself, and that we all have an obligation to listen carefully and communicate honestly.

Students will have discovered that we all respond to beauty and that, throughout history, people in every culture have been wonderfully expressive through the arts. Students will know that we all are members of groups, beginning with a family, which shape our lives and which we, in turn, can shape.

All students will begin to understand just how wonderful it is that we can recall our past and anticipate the future. They will know, too, that we can look around us and place ourselves in space. They will have learned that everyone needs to work, that work gives dignity to life, and they will have learned that we all consume things. They will start to know, as well, the importance of not wasting the precious resources we've been given.

Basic School students will have begun to understand that we're all part of the natural world, which gives us breath and life, and that, through discipline and study, we can learn about how nature works. Finally, those who leave the Basic School will have begun to think about how, through work and service, we give meaning to our lives, how all of us need to live with purpose.

Shortly before his death, the Jewish leader Abraham Joshua Heschel was asked what message he had for young people. He replied: "I would say: Let them remember that there is a meaning beyond absurdity. Let them be sure that every little deed counts, that every word has power, and that we can—every one—do our share to redeem the world in spite of all absurdities and all frustrations and all disappointments. And above all, remember that the meaning of life is to build a life as if it were a work of art."[7]

The Basic School is about helping each child build a life as if it were a work of art.

APPENDICES

APPENDIX A: FURTHER ACKNOWLEDGMENTS

The Carnegie Foundation gratefully acknowledges the following colleagues for their work in *The Basic School*:

BACKGROUND RESEARCH AND PAPERS

Connie Amon
Mary Ellen Bafumo
Richard Benjamin
Bret Birdsong
Anne Bridgman
Betty Watts Carrington
Ann Cook
Dale Coye
Virginia Edwards
Julie Freedman
John E. Gallagher
Lauren Maidment Green
Denise O'Neil Green
David Greenberg
Judy Grew
J. Eugene Haas
Sara Hanhan
Mary Harbaugh

Jan Hempel
Mary Taylor Huber
Lynn Jenkins
Gene I. Maeroff
Lorre Mendleson
Lee Mitgang
Ingrid Canright Morgan
Vito Perrone
Sally Reed
Katie Rubin
R. Craig Sautter
Karen Sykes
Jennifer Stoffel
Laura Taxel
Isabelle Tourneau
David Twenhafel
Lisa Wenner
Mark Whitaker

EARLY SITE VISITS

Maja Apelman
Mary E. Baldwin
Marguerite B. Bougere
Donna Bryant
Lucianne B. Carmichael
Marilyn M. Cohn
Ann Cook
Kathleen Devaney
Brenda S. Engel
William R. (Rod) Fielder
Ruth Goodenough

Robert Houston
Karla Smart Kadruas
Helen LaMar
Beth Lerman
Nancy Lesko
Catherine E. Loughlin
Ruth Ann Olson
Roberta Richardson
Lauren Sosniak
Ida Santos Stewart
Joseph H. Suina

SEMINARS, 1988

Helen Blank
Gilson Brown
Bettye Caldwell
Bea Cameron
Robert Chase
Edward A. Chittenden
Constance Clayton
Hubert Dyasi
David Elkind
Howard Gardner
David Hornbeck
Greg Humphrey

Lilian Katz
Kenneth Keniston
Catherine Loughlin
G. Niobe Marshall
Deborah Meier
Myriam Met
Aurelio Montemayor
Donald Moore
Ann Rosewater
Samuel Sava
Manya Ungar
Edward Zigler

SEMINAR ON EARLY EDUCATION, FEBRUARY 1991

Joan Almon
David Alsop
Henry Barnes
Carletta Bell
N. (Frederick) Brown
Patricia J. Bolaños
Bettye M. Caldwell
Janet Chladek
Marilyn Cohn
John Ellis

Patsy Kanter
Catherine Loughlin
Lorraine Merrick
Anne B. Norford
Rene Querido
Eugene Schwartz
Ken Smith
Sharon Smith
Betty Staley

TEACHER CONSULTANTS, APRIL 1991

Judy Buchanan
Carolyn Robinson

Lynne Strieb

SEMINAR ON ASSESSMENT, MAY 1991

Joan Boykoff Baron
Edward A. Chittenden

Mara Krechevsky
James Wilsford

MEETING ON THE EARLY YEARS
CHIEF STATE SCHOOL OFFICERS, MARCH 1993

Lois Adams-Rodgers
  Kentucky
Beth Aune
  Minnesota
Steven Barr
  Missouri

Barbara Baseggio
  California
Diane Bishop
  Arizona
Darlene Bolig
  Delaware

JoAnn Carter
Maryland
Harriet A. Egertson
Nebraska
Harriett Feldlaufer
Connecticut
Paul Fine
Delaware
Pascal D. Forgione, Jr.
Delaware
Linda Gerstle
Massachusetts
Kay Logan
Colorado
Nebraska Mays
Tennessee
Anita McClanahan
Oregon

Richard Ferguson
president, ACT
John MacDonald,
coordinator, Council of
Chief State School
Officers
Cyndie Schmeiser
vice president, ACT
Maris Vinovskis
U.S. Department
of Education

CARNEGIE TEACHER FELLOWS, SUMMER 1993

Marta Amezquita
San Antonio, Texas
Lillian Augustine
Perth Amboy, New Jersey
Frances Harmon
Upland, California
Nancy McCullum
Eugene, Oregon
Jean Mumper
New Paltz, New York

Eugene Schwartz
Spring Valley, New York
Kristin Sonquist
Minneapolis, Minnesota
Joy Warner
Charlotte, North Carolina
Suzann Westermann
San Antonio, Texas

PRINCIPALS, CORE NETWORK BASIC SCHOOLS, 1994–95

Lillian Brinkley
The Willard Model School
Norfolk, Virginia

Celia Burger
Irving Weber Elementary
Iowa City, Iowa

Sister Eleanor Daniels
Saint Ann's School
Somerville, Massachusetts

Joan Franks
Downtown Open School
Minneapolis, Minnesota

John Fries
David Cox Road Elementary
Charlotte, North Carolina

Arthur (Gus) Jacob
Center Elementary School
Kansas City, Missouri

Kae Everhart Keister
Benjamin Banneker Elementary
 School
Milford, Delaware

Linda Langiulli
Public School 207
New York, New York

Michelle Lufkins
Tiospa Zina Tribal School
Agency Village, South Dakota

William (Dudley) Reaves
William Perry Elementary
Waynesboro, Virginia

James Rodenmayer
Etna Road Elementary
Whitehall, Ohio

Alicia Thomas
Jackson-Keller Elementary
San Antonio, Texas

James Winger
Danebo Elementary School
Eugene, Oregon

APPENDIX B: TECHNICAL NOTES

INTERNATIONAL SCHOOLING PROJECT, 1994

The Carnegie Foundation for the Advancement of Teaching and the George H. Gallup International Institute jointly conducted an international study of primary school education. Surveys were administered in the late spring and early summer of 1994 by Gallup affiliate organizations in twelve countries including: Chile, China, (West) Germany, Great Britain, Israel, Italy, Japan, Mexico, Russia, Turkey, the United States, and Zimbabwe.

In each country, a questionnaire was administered to three populations:

- students age 9, 10, or 11 attending a primary school;
- parents of primary school children age 9, 10, or 11; and
- teachers of primary school students age 9, 10, or 11.

Approximately 500 students, 500 parents, and 350 teachers were interviewed in each country.

Separate questionnaires were developed for each of the three study groups, and, with translation, identical questionnaires were used in all countries. Many of the same questions were asked on each of the three survey instruments, so that issues may be compared not only internationally, but also across the three populations.

Questions on the survey instruments address many issues, including teachers and teaching, curriculum, the school climate, home-school connections, and social supports of education.

NATIONAL SURVEY OF KINDERGARTEN TEACHERS, 1991

The Carnegie Foundation for the Advancement of Teaching's National Survey of Kindergarten Teachers was administered by The Wirthlin Group of McLean, Virginia. The purpose of this research effort was to record the opinions of kindergarten teachers regarding the school readiness of children who entered their classes in the fall of 1990. In August 1991, questionnaires were mailed to 20,684 kindergarten teachers in all fifty states. Responses were received from 7,141 teachers, which represents a completion rate of 34.5 percent.

A stratified random sample design was used for this survey. Teachers' names were drawn from alphabetized lists of public school kindergarten teachers employed in each state. Market Data Retrieval of Shelton, Connecticut, maintains the lists, which include the names of approximately 75 percent of all public school teachers in the United States.

Using a fixed sample size from each state does not allow for differences between states in terms of the total population of kindergarten teachers. A weighting scheme was used so that the survey response would represent the relative numbers of teachers in the fifty states.

The short questionnaire included questions about the school readiness of children. Questions focused on the proportion of students who entered the classroom during the previous autumn not ready to participate in formal learning. Teachers were also asked how serious problems were in six specific dimensions of readiness and how the school readiness of children has changed over time.

Many of the results from the 1991 National Survey of Kindergarten Teachers appear in the 1991 Carnegie publication *Ready to Learn: A Mandate for the Nation*, by Ernest L. Boyer.

NATIONAL SURVEY OF ELEMENTARY SCHOOL PRINCIPALS, 1990

The National Survey of Elementary School Principals was administered by mail in 1990. Responses were received from 560 principals.

Questions asked for information about the grade levels and enrollment of the school, the school supplies and technology available for teaching, the use of standardized testing, the services available to students, parental involvement, and school control over decision-making.

SURVEY OF FIFTH- AND EIGHTH-GRADE STUDENTS, 1988

The Survey of Fifth- and Eighth-Grade Students was administered in the fall of 1988 by The Carnegie Foundation. Questionnaires were completed by 2,750 fifth-grade students and 2,906 eighth-grade students. Students from thirty school districts in seven states were included in the study. They were asked to respond to questions about their preferences for school subjects, about coping with personal problems, their feelings about the environments in which they live, and their participation in activities beyond the classroom.

SURVEY ON SCHOOL REFORM, 1988

The 1988 National Survey on School Reform questionnaire was mailed in the fall of 1987 to the same sample of 40,000 public school teachers as the 1987 National Survey of Public School Teachers. The focus of this survey effort was to learn how teachers perceived change in the school environment since widespread reform began in 1983. A total of 13,576 teachers returned questionnaires for an overall completion rate of 33.9 percent.

A stratified random sample design was used. Teachers' names were drawn from alphabetized lists of public school teachers employed in each state. Market Data Retrieval of Shelton, Connecticut, maintains these lists, which include the names of approximately 75 percent of all public school teachers in the United States.

Every "*n*th" name was drawn from the lists, where "*n*" was determined to achieve a total sample size of 800 teachers for each state. Because the alphabetical order of names would not be expected to have any relationship to the substance of the responses, the total sample size is composed of simple random samples from each state.

Again, using a fixed sample size from each state does not allow for differences between states in terms of the total population of teachers. We used a weighting scheme so that the survey response would represent the relative numbers of teachers in the fifty states, and we also calculated weights to reflect the true proportion of teachers from the elementary and secondary levels.

A complete summary of the results of the 1988 National Survey on School Reform, entitled *Report Card on School Reform: The Teachers Speak*, is available from The Carnegie Foundation.

NATIONAL SURVEY OF PUBLIC SCHOOL TEACHERS, 1987

The Carnegie Foundation for the Advancement of Teaching conducted the National Survey of Public School Teachers in 1987. The study was administered by The Wirthlin Group of McLean, Virginia. The purpose of this research effort was to gather data covering a wide range of topics related to the teaching profession. Questionnaires were mailed to 40,000 public elementary and secondary school teachers in all fifty states in the spring of 1987. Usable responses were received from 21,698 teachers, which represents a completion rate of 54.3 percent. The details of this survey and the 1988 Survey on School Reform are reported in the Foundation's technical report *The Condition of Teaching: A State-by-State Analysis, 1988*.

A stratified random sample design was used. Teachers' names were drawn from alphabetized lists of public school teachers employed in each state. Market Data Retrieval of Shelton, Connecticut, maintains these lists, which include the names of approximately 75 percent of all public school teachers in the United States.

Every "*n*th" name was drawn from the lists, where "*n*" was determined to achieve a total sample size of 800 teachers for each state. Because the alphabetical order of names would not be expected to have any relationship to the substance of the responses, the total sample size is composed of simple random samples from each state.

Since a fixed sample size from each state does not allow for differences between states in terms of the total population of teachers, a weighting scheme was developed so that the survey response would represent the relative numbers of teachers in the fifty states. Weights were calculated, as well, to reflect the true proportion of teachers from the elementary and secondary levels.

For additional information on the data presented in this report, contact The Carnegie Foundation for the Advancement of Teaching, 5 Ivy Lane, Princeton, New Jersey 08540.

Notes

Preface

1. Ernest L. Boyer, "Commissioner's Model for the 1980's," *The New York Times*, 7 January 1979, 5–6.

2. Ernest L. Boyer and Martin Kaplan, *Educating for Survival* (New York: Change Magazine Press, 1977).

3. Ernest L. Boyer and Arthur Levine, *A Quest for Common Learning: The Aims of General Education* (Princeton, NJ: The Carnegie Foundation for the Advancement of Teaching, 1981), 19.

4. Ernest L. Boyer, *High School: A Report on Secondary Education in America* (New York: Harper & Row, 1983), 95.

5. Boyer, *College: The Undergraduate Experience in America* (1987), 91.

6. Boyer, *Ready to Learn: A Mandate for the Nation* (Princeton, NJ: The Carnegie Foundation for the Advancement of Teaching, 1991), 12.

7. Over the years, there have been various translations of this quote. The American Indian College Fund in New York cites 1877 as the date of the quote, the year Sitting Bull led the Sioux into Canada and the United States government sent a commission to meet with him there. It is believed, however, that Sitting Bull may also have said this while appearing before the U.S. Senate Select Committee to Examine the Condition of Indian Tribes in Montana and the Dakotas, Standing Rock, MT, August 1883, according to a personal communication with staff at Salish Kootenai College, Pablo, MT, 30 March 1995, and documents at

the Newberry Library in Chicago. "While we have been unable to find the original source, it is a sentence, a theme that runs throughout Sitting Bull's whole life," states Robert M. Utley, author of *The Lance and the Shield: The Life and Times of Sitting Bull* (New York: Henry Holt and Company, 1993), personal communication, 31 July 1995.

Prologue: A New Beginning

1. W. Vance Grant, personal communication, U.S. Department of Education, National Center for Education Statistics, 25 July 1995.

2. Market Data Retrieval, personal communication, Weston, CT, 7 March 1995.

3. Ashley Montagu, *Growing Young*, 2d ed. (New York: Bergin and Garvey, 1989), 121.

4. Richard W. Riley, "State of American Education," remarks at Georgetown University, Washington, DC, 15 February 1994, 2.

5. Unless otherwise indicated, all quotes of teachers in this report come from personal interviews and The Carnegie Foundation surveys of teachers, 1990–95.

6. Peter F. Drucker, "The Age of Social Transformation," *The Atlantic Monthly*, November 1994, 64.

7. William J. Bennett, U.S. Department of Education, *First Lessons: A Report on Elementary Education in America* (Washington, DC: GPO, 1986).

8. Gabriela Mistral, *Llamado por el Niño (The Call for the Child)*, 1946. Various translations have been made of this work. The Nobel Prize winner, a Chilean poet and educator, first recited this prose in a worldwide radio broadcast of the United Nations calling on people in all countries to contribute a day's salary for the benefit of children. This is believed to be the beginning of

UNICEF, the United Nations International Children's Emergency Fund; Reynaldo C. Aguirre, the Library of Congress, personal communication, 27 July 1995.

A Shared Vision

1. "The need for community is universal. A sense of belonging, of continuity, of being connected to others and to ideas and values that make our lives meaningful and significant—these needs are shared by all of us." Thomas J. Sergiovanni, *Building Community in Schools* (San Francisco, CA: Jossey-Bass, 1994), xiii.

2. Unless otherwise indicated, all descriptions of schools are based on school visits and personal interviews, 1993–95.

3. "A sense of place is an ingredient common to almost all definitions of community. The group must exist in a definable space, and its geography and architecture feed its sense of belonging together. The shared knowledge that the sun in June will rise over that precise notch on the hill creates a climate of uniqueness: for no other group will the sun rise in quite that way." Robert V. Hine, *Community on the American Frontier: Separate But Not Alone* (Norman, OK: University of Oklahoma Press, 1985), 21.

4. "Small schools encourage teachers to innovate and 'take ownership of the curriculum.' Small school size improves students' outcomes on grades and test scores; . . . Security improves, violence decreases." Michael Klonsky, "Small Schools: The Numbers Tell the Story," Small Schools Workshop, College of Education, University of Illinois at Chicago, December 1994, 2 (manuscript); see also Marvin Martin, "Schools Offer a New Perspective: In Alternative Program, Less Equals More for Pupils," *Education Today*, special supplement, *Chicago Tribune*, 20 November 1994.

    "Small elementary schools show reasonably consistent and

positive learning effects. Perhaps the main reason is that the main agents of learning, teachers and students, undistracted by departmentalization and hierarchy, can concentrate on substance. Parents, too, are more likely to know the principal and teachers, be informed about their children's progress, participate more fully in school activities, and influence decision making." Herbert J. Walberg and Herbert J. Walberg III, "Losing Local Control," *Educational Researcher* 23, no. 5 (June/July 1994), 19–26; reprinted in Educational Excellence Network, *Network News and Views*, August 1994, 25.

A report from the University of Chicago notes that recent reform efforts in Chicago schools have worked best in smaller schools. "Small schools have been shown to be conducive to better relationships and communication among the students, teachers, principals, and parents," according to Anthony Bryk, who headed the study. "A smaller administrative unit facilitates the establishment of a strong school community." "Bryk Reports Principals' Perspective on School Reform," *University of Chicago Chronicle*, 10 December 1992; see also Anthony S. Bryk et al., *A View from the Elementary Schools: The State of Reform in Chicago*, a Report on the Steering Committee Consortium on Chicago School Research, July 1993.

"[S]chool size . . . was the key in the performance of students. Children do better in places small enough that 'the principal knows the name of each student.'" Dirk Johnson, "Study Says Small Schools Are Key to Learning," *The New York Times*, 21 September 1994, sec. B, 12; see also American Legislative Exchange Council, *The Report Card on American Education, 1993*, Washington, DC, September 1993.

5.   Winifred Gallagher, *The Power of Place: How Our Surroundings Shape Our Thoughts, Emotions, and Actions* (New York: Poseidon Press, 1993), 159.

6.   This is in keeping with the recommendations of elementary school principals. Responding to a national survey, 47 percent of

the elementary school principals said they considered three hundred to five hundred students the ideal number for the Basic School, and 38 percent suggested that the school have fewer than three hundred; National Association of Elementary School Principals, Principals' Opinion Survey, The Basic School Concept, 1990.

7.   Sara Snyder Crumpacker and James P. Esposito, "Designing Schools That Work," *The American School Board Journal* (February 1993), 49.

8.   Mary Erina Driscoll, "The Foundation of Community in Public Schools: Findings and Hypotheses," *Administrator's Notebook* 34, no. 4 (1990), 1.

9.   Thomas J. Sergiovanni, *Leadership for the Schoolhouse: How Is It Different? Why Is It Important?* (San Francisco, CA: Jossey-Bass, 1995).

10.   Daniel U. Levine and Lawrence W. Lezotte, *Unusually Effective Schools: A Review and Analysis of Research and Practice*, The National Center for Effective Schools, Madison, WI, 1990, 21.

11.   Paul T. Hill, Gail E. Foster, and Tamar Gendler, *High Schools with Character*, Rand Corporation, Santa Monica, CA, August 1990, 35–38.

12.   "Just as personal visions are pictures or images people carry in their heads and hearts, so too are shared visions pictures that people throughout an organization carry. They create a sense of commonality that permeates the organization and gives coherence to diverse activities. . . . When people truly share a vision, they are connected, bound together by a common aspiration. . . . Shared visions derive their power from a common caring." Peter M. Senge, *The Fifth Discipline: The Art and Practice of the Learning Organization* (New York: Doubleday, 1990), 206.

13.   Wayne C. Booth, "Mere Rhetoric, Rhetoric, and the Search for Common Learning," in *Common Learning: A Carnegie*

Colloquium on General Education (Washington, DC: The Carnegie Foundation for the Advancement of Teaching, 1981), 54.

14. In their study, *Failing at Fairness*, Myra and David Sadker argue that in elementary classrooms today girls receive "hidden lessons." They are called on less often, receive less attention, praise, and help from teachers. This has a direct impact on student achievement; Myra Sadker and David Sadker, *Failing at Fairness: How America's Schools Cheat Girls* (New York: Charles Scribner's Sons, 1994), ix, 1–4.

15. See U.S. General Accounting Office, *School Age Demographics: Recent Trends Pose New Educational Challenges*, Briefing Report to Congressional Requesters, Washington, DC, August 1993; and Educational Research Service, ERS *Report: Demographic Factors in American Education*, Arlington, VA, 1995.

16. Concerns about discipline are increasing, even in the lower grades. For six years in a row, parents have responded to opinion polls by saying that discipline is the biggest problem facing public schools; Stanley M. Elam, Lowell C. Rose, and Alec M. Gallup, "The 26th Annual Phi Delta Kappa/Gallup Poll of the Public's Attitudes Toward the Public Schools," *Phi Delta Kappan* 76 (September 1994), 43–45.

17. David Elkind, interviewed by Jean Seligmann, "How Parents Can Talk to Their Kids," *Newsweek*, 10 January 1994, 50.

18. A recent survey found that a large majority of Americans, in all parts of the country and across every demographic category, say that too many public schools are not providing a safe, orderly environment, the basic underpinning for a sound education; Jean Johnson and John Immerwahr, *First Things First: What Americans Expect from the Public Schools*, Public Agenda Foundation, 1994, 10.

19. Hill, Foster, and Gendler, *High Schools with Character*.

20. Richard L. Curwin and Allen N. Mendler explore the idea of the social contract in schools, in "The Social Contract," *Discipline*

with Dignity, Association for Supervision and Curriculum Development, Alexandria, VA, 1988, 47–64.

21. Mary E. Clark, "Meaningful Social Bonding as a Universal Human Need," in *Conflict: Human Needs Theory*, ed. John Burton (New York: St. Martin's Press, 1990), 44.

22. *"Technos* Interview with James P. Comer, M.D.," *Technos* 1, no. 4 (winter 1992), 5; full interview 4–7.

23. Evidence suggests many children today are lonely, that they are less connected to the adult world than in the past and spend less time with the older generations. One study by a University of Maryland sociologist found that parents spend an average of only seventeen hours per week with their children, compared to thirty in 1965; Amitai Etzioni, "Children of the Universe," *Utne Reader*, May/June 1993, 57; from Amitai Etzioni, *The Spirit of Community: Rights, Responsibilities and the Communitarian Agenda* (New York: Crown Publishers, 1993).

Another study, by Victor Fuchs, a Stanford University economist, found that the time parents have available to children fell appreciably between 1960 and 1986—ten hours less per week; Victor R. Fuchs, *Women's Quest for Economic Equality* (Cambridge, MA: Harvard University Press, 1988), 111; see also Barbara Dafoe Whitehead, "The New Family Values," *Utne Reader*, May/June 1993, 63, citing Sylvia Ann Hewlett, *When the Bough Breaks: The Cost of Neglecting Our Children* (New York: Basic Books, 1991), 15, 73.

24. The Carnegie Foundation for the Advancement of Teaching, Survey of Fifth- and Eighth-Graders, 1988.

25. National Association of Secondary School Principals, "NASSP, Community of Caring Initiate Partnership to Teach Students Values," press release, Reston, VA, 3 February 1995, 1.

26. In a study of communities, researchers found that "celebrations play a central role in building and sustaining community." Carolyn R. Shaffer and Kristin Anundsen, *Creating Community*

Anywhere: Finding Support and Connection in a Fragmented World (New York: Jeremy P. Tarcher/Perigee Books, 1993), 305–308.

27.   Alex Kotlowitz, remarks at the Blue Ribbon Schools Program ceremony, U.S. Department of Education, Washington, DC, 13 May 1993; see also Alex Kotlowitz, *There Are No Children Here: The Story of Two Boys Growing Up in the Other America* (New York: Doubleday, 1991).

Teachers as Leaders

1.   In analyzing what made 212 successful elementary schools work, researchers concluded that "effective leadership is central to a school's success. While a school's leadership stems essentially from the principal, other professionals in the school also can provide strong leadership, depending on the principal's delegation skills. While the importance of leadership is clear, individual leadership styles vary markedly from one school to another, with the style arising within the context of the particular school. What most characterizes effective school leaders is their ability to set and maintain clear direction for the school while facilitating the work of the staff." Bruce L. Wilson and Thomas B. Corcoran, "A Look at 212 Successful Schools," *Streamlined Seminar* 7, no. 1, National Association of Elementary School Principals, September 1988, 2–3; and overview of a report from Research for Better Schools, *Places Where Children Succeed: A Profile of Outstanding Public Elementary Schools*, Philadelphia, PA, 1987.

2.   Jack McCurdy, *The Role of the Principal in Effective Schools: Problems & Solutions*, an AASA Critical Issues Report, American Association of School Administrators, Arlington, VA, 1989.

"While the teacher is the person who establishes the climate for the classroom, it is the principal who is the force that sets the tone and provides the drive, who clarifies the belief system of the school, who models the values, and who reinforces the staff as they seek to improve instruction. Best School principals really believe that 'we can get it right in this school, for every kid.'" Evelyn Hunt Ogden and Vito Germinario, *The Nation's Best Schools: Blueprints for Excellence,* Volume 1, Elementary and Middle Schools (Lancaster, PA: Technomic Publishing Co., 1994), 10.

3. Harold Howe II, *Thinking about Our Kids: An Agenda for American Education* (New York: The Free Press, 1993), 130.

4. Lillian Brinkley, personal communication, August 1994.

5. In a survey of teachers about their attitudes toward school reform, only 41 percent of teachers report that school-based management, "in which teachers are given more say in school decision making," has had a "major impact" on their school. The remaining 59 percent say this basic reform has not made a major impact on the schools in which they teach. Louis Harris and Robert F. Wagner, Jr., *Testing Assumptions: A Survey of Teachers' Attitudes Toward the Nation's School Reform Agenda*, a study conducted by LH Research for the Ford Foundation, New York, NY, September 1993, iv.

    The Committee for Economic Development, a business group, has argued that schools are actually ailing from an overload of mandates imposed on them and suggests that schools should have more authority over funding, curriculum, teaching, and hiring or firing, while meeting specified achievement goals; Committee for Economic Development, *Putting Learning First: Governing and Managing the Schools for High Achievement: An Executive Summary*, New York, NY, September 1994.

6. Michael W. Kirst, "A Changing Context Means School Board Reform," *Phi Delta Kappan* 75 (January 1994), 378–81.

    Elementary schools "feel cut off from a sense of professionalism by their perceived lack of autonomy," according to a California report. "In too many school districts, . . . decisions that directly affect what takes place in the classroom—which topics will be taught, which textbooks will be used, how classes will be scheduled, and how a teacher's performance will be measured—are made elsewhere." Elementary Grades Task Force and the California Department of Education, *It's Elementary!* Elementary Grades Task Force Report, Sacramento, CA, 1992, 53.

7.   John I. Goodlad, "Schooling: Issues and Answers," *Ideals in Transition: Tomorrow's America*, special magazine section, *St. Louis Post-Dispatch*, Centennial Edition, 25 March 1979, 72.

8.   "Effective teaching is complicated and difficult. It usually requires information, expertise, and support far beyond the resources available to the individual teacher working alone in an isolated classroom. Teachers who collaborate with their colleagues are more likely to be effective with students, because they will benefit from expanded resources." Fred M. Newmann, "School-wide Professional Community," *Issues in Restructuring Schools*, Center on Organization and Restructuring of Schools, Madison, WI, issue report no. 6, spring 1994, 1.

9.   Robert Spillane, personal communication, September 1993.

10.   Lack of noninstructional time for teachers may be one of the chief reasons our elementary schools have failed to emerge as institutions ready for the twenty-first century. A recent report from the Rand Corporation called *Time for Reform* suggests that school reformers have not paid enough serious attention to providing school personnel with the time needed to plan, implement new programs, and refine old approaches. Teachers do not have time to attend workshops, practice new teaching methods, or receive feedback, researchers found; Susanna Purnell and Paul Hill, *Time for Reform*, Rand Corporation, Santa Monica, CA, 1992.

11.   A study of Japanese teachers found that elementary teachers there are provided a longer school year and more time in the school day—as much as half the day—in which to prepare for daily lessons, share ideas with one another, and design curriculum; F. Howard Nelson and Timothy O'Brien, *How U.S. Teach-*

ers Measure Up Internationally: A Comparative Study of Teacher Pay, Training, and Conditions of Service, American Federation of Teachers, Washington, DC, July 1993, 8, 25–29, 37–38.

12. Purnell and Hill, *Time for Reform*; see also Annette Licitra, "Rand Report Explores Ways to Free Time for School Reform," *Education Daily*, 3 December 1992, 1, 3; and Meg Sommerfeld, "More Planning Time Urged for Front-Line School Reformers," *Education Week*, 9 December 1992, 8.

13. A recent study of Kentucky schools found that teachers aren't even given adequate time to make the changes mandated by the 1990 Kentucky Education Reform Act. In the attempt to implement ungraded classrooms (just one of the reforms), kindergarten through third-grade teachers spent 305 hours of their own time during the school year, while the school districts provided only ten hours of released time for professional development and planning. Appalachia Educational Laboratory, Inc., *Finding Time for School Reform: Obstacles and Answers*, a joint study by the Kentucky Education Association and AEL, Charleston, WV, March 1993.

14. Gene I. Maeroff, *The Empowerment of Teachers: Overcoming the Crisis of Confidence* (New York: Teachers College Press, 1988), 26.

15. Paul A. Gagnon, "Everything But Time," *History Matters!* National Council for History Education, Inc. (April 1995), 2, 6.

16. In a 1990 survey, The Basic School Concept, the National Association of Elementary School Principals found that 48 percent of principals surveyed believed that the teacher's day should be lengthened to include time for training and planning. Sixty-six percent said that involving teachers in planning and design of the curriculum and in the operation of the school would help teachers be more effective. Many principals suggested adding two weeks to the year for teachers to plan and train.

17. Based on school visits; see also North Central Regional Educational Laboratory, "Professional Development: Changing Times,"

Policy Briefs, report 4, Oak Brook, IL, 1994; and Mary Anne Raywid, "Finding Time for Collaboration," *Educational Leadership* (September 1993), 30–34.

18. Patricia Bolaños, principal, Key School, Indianapolis, IN, personal communication, October 1994.

19. James Winger, personal communication, May 1994.

20. Jeffrey N. Lobel, personal communication, Blue Ribbon Schools Program ceremony, U.S. Department of Education, Washington, DC, September 1993.

21. Theodore Sizer, remarks, seminar on the New Standards Project, Chicago, IL, May 1993; also Coalition of Essential Schools, Brown University, Providence, RI, publications.

22. John I. Goodlad, "A Study of Schooling: Some Implications for School Improvement," *Phi Delta Kappan* 64 (April 1983), 557.

23. For more information on standards for working with young children, see Sue Bredekamp, ed., *Developmentally Appropriate Practice in Early Childhood Programs Serving Children from Birth Through Age 8*, expanded edition, National Association for the Education of Young Children, Washington, DC, 1986.

24. The Walt Disney Company and The Disney Channel, The American Teacher Awards, 1991, press release.

25. Linda Darling-Hammond, "Will 21st-Century Schools Really Be Different?" *Education Digest* (September 1994), 4; originally published in *Virginia Journal of Education* 87 (March 1994), 6–13.

26. American school districts spend, on average, less than 0.5 percent of their funds on staff development, compared to up to 10 percent of school expenditures in other countries, according to recent research on the status of teaching in the United States; Linda Darling-Hammond, "The Current Status of Teaching and Teacher Development in the United States," report prepared for the National Commission on Teaching and America's Future, November 1994, 15.

27. Hillary Foliart, personal communication, June 1995; and Exxon Corporation and Exxon Education Foundation, "Professional Practice School Program," *". . . We Were Only Limited by Our Imagination and Creativity,"* Irving, TX, 1994, 24–27.

28. Disney Company, American Teacher Awards, 1991, press release; and Cyrilla Hergenhan, personal communication, 27 March 1995.

Parents as Partners

1. Richard W. Riley, remarks at the National Press Club, Washington, DC, 7 September 1994; see also U.S. Department of Education, *Strong Families, Strong Schools: Building Community Partnerships for Learning* (Washington, DC: GPO, September 1994).

2. Samuel G. Sava, "Post Script: On Slowing Down," *Principal* 73, no. 5 (May 1994), 64.

3. Study after study links parent involvement to the reading achievement of youngsters and to increased test scores in math. But researchers have also found that involving parents in their children's schooling has a positive impact on a child's behavior and attitudes about school; ERIC Clearinghouse, *Value Search: Parent Involvement in the Educational Process* (Eugene, OR: ERIC Clearinghouse on Educational Management, 1993).

   In a review of research covering the last two decades, Joyce L. Epstein has also found that parent involvement not only improves student achievement, it also improves teacher practices; Joyce L. Epstein, "Effects on Student Achievement of Teachers' Practices of Parent Involvement," *Advances in Reading/ Language Research* 5, 261–76; and Joyce L. Epstein, "School and Family Partnerships," *Encyclopedia of Educational Research* 4, 6th ed., ed. Marvin C. Alkin (New York: Macmillan, 1992), 1139–51.

4.   Metropolitan Life Insurance Company and Louis Harris and Associates, Inc., *The Metropolitan Life Survey of the American Teacher 1993: Teachers Respond to President Clinton's Education Proposals*, MetLife, New York, NY, 1993, 17.

5.   Stanley M. Elam, Lowell C. Rose, and Alec M. Gallup, "The 25th Annual Phi Delta Kappa/Gallup Poll of the Public's Attitudes Toward the Public Schools," *Phi Delta Kappan* 75 (October 1993), 149.

6.   Arlie Hochschild, *The Second Shift: Working Parents and the Revolution at Home* (New York: Viking, 1989), 231, 267; quoted in Robert N. Bellah et al., *The Good Society* (New York: Alfred A. Knopf, 1991), 48.

7.   See Jeff Meade, "Prodigal Parents: To Succeed, Schools Must Reach Out and Bring Parents In," *Teacher Magazine*, May–June 1992, 17. See also Terrel H. Bell, "Reflections One Decade After *A Nation at Risk*," *Phi Delta Kappan* 74 (April 1993), 592–97.

8.   Keith Geiger, "A Shared Responsibility," National Education Association advertisement, *Education Week*, 16 February 1994, 15.

9.   Stephanie Hoover, personal communication, 7 March 1995; see also "Snapshot: Cradle School at Byck Elementary," *Instructor* 99 (March 1990), 54.

10.   Ken Plumley, personal communication, Office of the Governor, Springfield, MA, 7 February 1995; see also remarks as delivered by Gov. William F. Weld before the Committee on Educational Policy, Worcester, MA, 24 October 1991.

11.   Michael Charney and Cleveland Teachers Union, personal communication, 3 February 1995; see also Michael Charney, "Parent Involvement in Cleveland," *Rethinking Schools* 7, no. 3 (spring 1993), 5.

12.   Merry White, *The Japanese Educational Challenge: A Commitment to Children* (New York: The Free Press, 1987), 111.

13. John Varis, personal communication, April 1995; see also materials from Reading Board of Education, Reading, OH, including "Reading Community Schools Memorandum of Understanding, 1992–93."

14. Kevin Duchschere, "Kids, Parents, School Officials All Cross Their Hearts at Rally," *Minneapolis Star Tribune*, 21 January 1994; and Minneapolis Public Schools, press release, 20 January 1994.

15. Researchers have found that the majority of school districts do not have any activities or programs to ease the transition of youngsters from preschool experiences to kindergarten; RMC Research Corp., "Transitions to Kindergarten in American Schools," report funded by the U.S. Department of Education, Office of Policy and Planning, 1992; in "Report Says Few Schools Promote Preschool-to-School Transition," *Report on Preschool Programs*, 6 May 1992, 91–92, and Deborah L. Cohen, "Study Finds Little Done to Ease Transition to School," *Education Week*, 22 April 1992, 4.

16. The student inventory we suggest is based on our analysis of parent entry forms and parent enrollment forms in thirty-five randomly selected elementary schools in ten states throughout the country. We discovered that most merely asked for basic health statistics. The only national form was the computerized one formerly used by the federally funded national Migrant Student Record Transfer System, based in Arkansas, that tracked the two million school children migrating seasonally across the United States. A few states are currently exploring a computerized form for their students as well.

17. Parents who receive frequent and positive messages from teachers tend to get more involved in their children's education than parents who do not receive such communications; Carole Ames, Madhab Khoju, and Thomas Watkins, *Parent Involvement: The Relationship Between School-to-Home Communication and Parents' Perceptions and Beliefs*, Center on Families, Commu-

nities, Schools, and Children's Learning, The Johns Hopkins University, Baltimore, MD, Report No. 15, March 1993.

18. Denise Lunsford, personal communication, 6 March 1995; see also nomination forms, 1993–94 Elementary Blue Ribbon Schools Program, sponsored by the U.S. Department of Education.

19. Joya Chatterjee, personal communication, 7 March 1995; see also nomination forms, 1993–94 Elementary Blue Ribbon Schools Program, sponsored by the U.S. Department of Education.

20. Vivian R. Johnson, *Parent/Family Centers: Dimensions of Functioning in 28 Schools in 14 States*, Center on Families, Communities, Schools, and Children's Learning, The Johns Hopkins University, Baltimore, MD, report no. 20, September 1993.

21. David Burke, personal communication, 7 March 1995; also State Farm Insurance Company, "State Farm Offers Employees Paid Time Off to Help in Schools," press release, Bloomington, IL, 7 February 1995.

22. Boyer, *Ready to Learn*, 73, citing Hal Morgan and Kerry Tucker, *Companies That Care* (New York: Simon and Schuster, 1991), 330–31, and Sandra Conway, NCNB, November 1991.

23. Charles Waters, *Hemmings Motor News*, personal communication, April 1995; and Boyer, *Ready to Learn*, 73–74.

24. California Department of Education, "New Law Allows Working Parents to Take Time Off to Help in Their Children's Schools," press release, 3 February 1995.

25. Southern Education Foundation, Inc., "Getting Involved: One Parent's Story," SEF *News* 7, no. 1, Atlanta, GA, February 1993, 7–8.

26. Susan R. Larabee, parent, personal communication, 10 August 1995.

The Centrality of Language

1. Steven Pinker, *The Language Instinct: How the Mind Creates Language* (New York: William Morrow and Company, 1994), 17.

2. Robert M. Augros and George N. Stanciu, *The New Story of Science: Mind and the Universe* (New York: Bantam Books, 1986), 39, citing Richard Feynman, *The Character of Physical Law* (Cambridge, MA: MIT Press, 1965), 171.

3. Ibid., citing Werner Heisenberg, "The Meaning of Beauty in the Exact Sciences," in *Across the Frontiers* (New York: Harper and Row, 1974), 183.

4. Victor Weisskopf (n.p., n.d.); quoted by Frank Press, president, National Academy of Sciences, Annual Meeting of Phi Beta Kappa Associates, 25 October 1986.

5. Pam Belluck, "At 15, Westinghouse Finalist Grasps 'Holy Grail' of Math," *The New York Times*, 25 January 1995, sec. A, 1.

6. The effective teaching of such basics, from the public's point of view, is not a trivial or inconsequential goal, according to a recent national survey. The public believes it is the foundation on which children build their futures. "Sixty percent of Americans say that 'not enough emphasis on the basics such as reading, writing, and math' is a serious problem in their local schools." At the same time, this finding does not imply that the public believes the teaching of such "basics" is at the exclusion of other, more challenging work or the development of higher order skills. "What most people seem to mean," researchers concluded, "is 'first things first.'" Jean Johnson and John Immerwahr, *First Things First: What Americans Expect from the Public Schools*, Public Agenda Foundation, New York, NY, 1994, 13–14.

The American Council for the Arts found that 91 percent of Americans say it is important for children to learn about the arts and develop artistic skills in schools; American Council for the Arts and LH Research (Louis Harris), "Americans Believe Arts Are Essential Part of Education," press release on *Americans and the Arts VI*, national public opinion survey on the arts, Washington, DC, 19 March 1992, 1–2.

7.   See Kurt W. Fischer and Arlyne Lazerson, *Human Development: From Conception Through Adolescence* (New York: W. H. Freeman and Company, 1984), 365.

8.   Mortimer J. Adler, *The Paideia Proposal: An Educational Manifesto* (New York: Macmillan, 1982), 50.

9.   Lillian R. Putnam, "Reading Instruction: What Do We Know Now That We Didn't Know Thirty Years Ago?" *Language Arts* 71 (September 1994), 363.

10. Estimates vary on the number of elementary teachers using the whole language approach. A recent survey by the U.S. Department of Education found that over 53 percent of first-grade students and 23 percent of third-grade students have teachers who use the whole language method. Michael J. Puma et al., *Prospects: The Congressionally Mandated Study of Educational Growth and Opportunity*, interim report, prepared by Abt Associates, Inc., Bethesda, MD, for the U.S. Department of Education, Planning and Evaluation Service, December 1994, 306.

A recent article in *The Atlantic Monthly* reported that the whole-language method is used by one-fifth of all teachers of reading, "with an even larger proportion adapting elements of it, such as the greater use of authentic children's literature and the decreased use of intensive phonics." And some form of whole-language ideology has been adopted by more than a dozen state education agencies; Art Levine, "The Great Debate Revisited," *The Atlantic Monthly*, December 1994, 41.

11. New Zealand Department of Education, *Reading in Junior Classes* (Wellington, New Zealand: Department of Education, 1985), 9.

12. A recent national report on student writing states that many American children have serious difficulty producing informative, persuasive, or narrative writing that would be considered effective. One of the main problems, researchers found, is that students simply do not spend enough time writing in school; Arthur N. Applebee et al., National Assessment of Educational Progress, NAEP *1992 Writing Report Card*, report prepared for the U.S. Department of Education, Office of Educational Research and Improvement, National Center for Education Statistics, June 1994.

13. Lucy McCormick Calkins, *Lessons from a Child: On the Teaching and Learning of Writing* (Exeter, NH: Heinemann Educational Books, 1983), 152-59; see also Fred M. Hechinger, "About Education: The Joy of Teaching Writing," *The New York Times*, 3 December 1985, sec. C, 16.

14. According to an organization called U.S. English, Inc., in Washington, DC, twenty-one states have passed legislation to make English their official language; Mindy Hess, personal communication, July 1995.

     English is the second officially recognized language in forty-four countries with a combined population of 1.6 billion people, one-third of the world's inhabitants. More than two-thirds of all scientific papers are published in English, two-thirds of business deals in Europe are conducted in English, 70 percent of the world's mail is sent in envelopes addressed in English; Bill Bryson, *The Mother Tongue: English and How It Got That Way* (New York: Avon Books, 1990).

15. C. Edward Scebold, American Council on the Teaching of Foreign Languages, personal communication, Yonkers, NY, 11 August 1995.

16. Eugene Garcia, of the U.S. Department of Education, notes that, although California and Texas have the largest population of new immigrants, the demographics are changing all across the

country. "The demographic realities suggest that now 5 percent to 10 percent of the students coming into schools do not speak English," says Garcia. "If you look down the road, we would expect 2025 to be the magical year, when the majority of students will come from backgrounds not speaking English." Jo Anna Natale, "Homeroom to the World," *The Executive Educator* (January 1994), 15.

17.   Boyer, *High School*, 100; unpublished data from Population Reference Bureau, Washington, DC. Also, more than seventeen million people in the United States currently speak Spanish today, ten times the number who speak French. More people in the United States speak Spanish than all other foreign languages combined, according to Josue Gonzalez, author of "Spanish as a Second School Language: Adding Language to the Discourse of Multicultural Education," *Reinventing Urban Education: Multiculturalism and the Social Context of Schooling*, ed. Francisco L. Rivera-Batiz, Institute for Urban Minority Education, Teachers College, Columbia University, 1994. By the year 2010, Hispanics are expected to become the largest minority group in the United States, according to a recent report from the Council for Educational Development and Research, *Schools Along the Border: The Educational Implications of* NAFTA, Washington, DC, 1994.

18.   Recent research in linguistics has found that people have a window of opportunity for learning foreign languages that peaks during the ages ten to thirteen, according to Lourdes Mallis, language professor at Keene State College in New Hampshire. This is the time when children are most often able to make new connections within their brain. Their tongue is still in an agile state for the formation of sounds, particularly sounds they have heard—the click of the tongue in African languages, the trill of the *R* in Spanish. At adolescence, learning a foreign language with native fluency and pronunciation becomes difficult, as many adult Americans have learned the hard way; Lourdes Mallis, personal communications, 1991–95.

In addition, other "researchers note the best time to teach students cultural studies is between the ages of seven and twelve, when children are less egocentric and can view themselves as part of a larger world," writes Susan Black in "Learning Languages," *The Executive Educator*, March 1993, 34.

19.   AMOCO Corporation, "First-Ever AMOCO Partner Award to Honor University of Chicago School Mathematics Project," press release, Chicago, IL, 28 July 1993, 3.

20.   In math, as in reading, we now know a lot more about how children learn. "Preschoolers are sophisticated about numbers and have learned more math than many parents or teachers realize," states John T. Bruer, president of the James S. McDonnell Foundation in St. Louis, which supports scientific and education research. "By age three, most children can count small sets of visible objects, and by age four or five, they can correct the counting mistakes others make. Most five-year-olds have also learned to compare two numbers for size." As a result, Mr. Bruer argues that the "elementary arithmetic curricula should build on and extend children's informal, preschool understanding of numbers." Researchers have found that knowing the "sense" behind the numbers increases student achievement in math; John T. Bruer, "How Children Learn," *The Executive Educator*, August 1994, 34.

21.   California State Department of Education, "Teaching for Understanding," *The Mathematics Model Curriculum Guide, Kindergarten Through Grade Eight* (Sacramento, CA: 1987), 12.

22.   Recently, the National Assessment of Educational Progress revealed that as many as two-thirds of the nation's students, including fourth-graders, are performing poorly on mathematics questions that require them to take time to reason and explain their answers. Only 16 percent of fourth-graders could answer mathematics questions requiring problem-solving skills. Only 23 percent of fourth-graders could explain who ate the greater portion of a pizza, even with the use of pictures; Ina V.S. Mullis

et al., *Executive Summary of the* NAEP *1992 Mathematics Report Card for the Nation and the States*, report prepared for the U.S. Department of Education, Office of Educational Research and Improvement, National Center for Education Statistics, April 1993.

23.   David Baumann, "NRC Turns Up Volume on Math Crisis," *Education Daily*, 11 April 1990, 2.

24.   California State Department of Education, *Mathematics Curriculum Guide*, 12.

25.   Charlene Luks, principal, personal communication, 13 April 1995; see also, nomination forms, 1993–94 Elementary Blue Ribbon Schools Program, sponsored by the U.S. Department of Education.

26.   Exxon Corporation and Exxon Education Foundation, "K–3 Mathematics," ". . . *We Were Only Limited By Our Imagination and Creativity*," Irving, TX, 1994, 6–9.

27.   Patte Barth and Ruth Mitchell, *Smart Start: Elementary Education for the 21st Century*, sponsored by The Council for Basic Education (Golden, CO: North American Press, 1992), 60.

28.   Elliot W. Eisner, personal communication, 29 July 1995; see also Elliot W. Eisner, "The Education of Vision," *Educational Horizons* 71 (winter 1993), 80–85; Eisner, "Rethinking Literacy," *Educational Horizons* 69 (spring 1991), 120–28; and Eisner "The Misunderstood Role of the Arts in Human Development," *Phi Delta Kappan* 73 (April 1992), 591–95.

29.   Howard Gardner, *Frames of Mind: The Theory of Multiple Intelligences* (New York: Basic Books, 1983).

30.   Jane Alexander, remarks to the Educational Press of America Association, annual meeting, Chicago, IL, 9 June 1994.

31.   Jerrold Ross and Ellyn Berk, "National Arts Education Research Center Principal Research Findings, 1987–1991," National Arts Education Research Center, New York University, 1992.

32. Ann Alejandro, "Like Happy Dreams—Integrating Visual Arts, Writing, and Reading," *Language Arts* 71 (January 1994), 13.

33. Literacy in the Arts Task Force, "Literacy in the Arts: An Imperative for New Jersey Schools," report prepared for the State of New Jersey, October 1989, 20; see also Eduardo Garcia, "The Lessons New Jersey Has Learned," *Teaching Theatre* 2, no. 1, Special Issue: The Theatre Curriculum (fall 1990), 17-19.

34. See nomination forms, 1991–92 Elementary Blue Ribbon Schools Program, sponsored by the U.S. Department of Education.

35. Lewis Thomas, *Late Night Thoughts on Listening to Mahler's Ninth Symphony* (New York: The Viking Press, 1983), 52.

The Core Commonalities

1. E. D. Hirsch, Jr., *Cultural Literacy: What Every American Needs to Know* (Boston, MA: Houghton Mifflin, 1987).

2. Albert Shanker, "Where We Stand: Disciplinary Learning," American Federation of Teachers advertisement, *The New York Times,* 5 February 1995, sec. E, 4.

3. Lionel Elvin, *The Place of Commonsense in Educational Thought* (London: George Allen and Unwin Ltd., 1977), 34; quoted in Heidi Hayes Jacobs, ed., *Interdisciplinary Curriculum: Design and Implementation* (Alexandria, VA: Association for Supervision and Curriculum Development, 1989), 1–2.

4. Mortimer J. Adler and Charles Van Doren, *How to Read a Book* (New York: Simon and Schuster, 1972), 270.

5. Renate Nummela Caine and Geoffrey Caine, *Making Connections: Teaching and The Human Brain* (Alexandria, VA: Association for Supervision and Curriculum Development, 1991); see also Caine and Caine, "Understanding a Brain-Based Approach to Learning and Teaching," *Educational Leadership* (October 1990), 66–70.

6. The "Core Commonalities" is the curriculum framework created and developed by Ernest L. Boyer, president, The Carnegie Foundation for the Advancement of Teaching, 1995.

7. Pablo Casals, *Joys and Sorrows* (New York: Simon and Schuster, 1970; Touchstone Book, 1974), 295.

8. Ralph Waldo Emerson, *Journals and Miscellaneous Notebooks of Ralph Waldo Emerson*, 1832, vol. 3, ed. William H. Gilman et al. (Cambridge, MA: Harvard University Press, 1960), 318–19.

9. Will Durant, *Our Oriental Heritage*, vol. 1 of *The Story of Civilization* (New York: Simon and Schuster, 1935; copyright renewed, 1963), 30.

10. T. S. Eliot, *Burnt Norton*, in *Four Quartets* (New York: Harcourt, Brace, Jovanovich, 1971), 13.

11. Murray Sidlin, "Someone's Priority," speech given at the Aspen Conference on the Talented and Gifted, sponsored by the U.S. Department of Health, Education, and Welfare, Office of the Gifted and Talented, Aspen, CO, June 1978.

12. Ella Wilcox, "Unlock the Joy of Music," *Education Digest* (January 1995), 67–69; condensed from *Teaching Music*, published by Music Educators National Conference, Reston, VA, 2 December 1994, 34–35, 46.

13. Frederick Ungar, ed., and Heinz Norden, trans., *Goethe's World View: Presented in His Reflections and Maxims* (New York: Frederick Ungar Publishing Co., 1963), 82–83; further translation by Eugene Schwartz.

14. Reinhold Niebuhr, *Moral Man and Immoral Society* (New York: Charles Scribner's Sons, 1952), 257; see also Reinhold Niebuhr, *The Nature and Destiny of Man: A Christian Interpretation*, vol. 2, *Human Destiny* (New York: Charles Scribner's Sons, 1964), 312.

15. Frances M. Barbour, *A Concordance to the Sayings in Franklin's "Poor Richard"* (Detroit, MI: Gale Research Co., 1974), 175,

citing December 1737; refers also to Burton Stevenson, ed., *The Home Book of Proverbs, Maxims, and Familiar Phrases* (New York, 1948).

16. Martin Luther King, Jr., *A Testament of Hope: The Essential Writings and Speeches of Martin Luther King, Jr.*, ed. James Melvin Washington (San Francisco, CA: Harper Collins, 1986), 265.

17. William Damon, *Greater Expectations: Overcoming the Culture of Indulgence in America's Homes and Schools* (New York: The Free Press, 1995), 39.

18. Mark Van Doren, *Liberal Education* (Boston, MA: Beacon Press, 1959), 115.

Measuring Results

1. "*Technos* Interview with Diane Ravitch," *Technos* 1, no. 4 (Fall 1992), 4; full interview 4–7.

2. Lynne Hall, Lynn Stuart, and Brenda Engel, eds., *The Cambridge Handbook of Documentation and Assessment: Child Portfolios and Teacher Records in the Primary Grades*, The North Dakota Study Group on Evaluation, University of North Dakota, Grand Forks, ND, 1995, 69.

3. Janet Price and Sara Schwabacher, with Ted Chittenden, *The Multiple Forms of Evidence Study: Assessing Reading Through Student Work Samples, Teacher Observations, and Tests*, NCREST Reprint Series, National Center for Restructuring Education, Schools, and Teaching, Teachers College, Columbia University, New York, NY, May 1993, 1, 21.

4. Howard Gardner, *Frames of Mind: The Theory of Multiple Intelligences* (New York: Basic Books, 1983).

5. See "Arts PROPEL Demonstrates High Quality Assessments," *Fair Test Examiner*, fall 1992, 10–13.

6. Jay McTighe and Steven Ferrara, *Assessing Learning in the Classroom*, a report prepared for the National Education Association, Professional Standards and Practice, November 1994, 4; see also John Ayto, *Dictionary of Word Origins* (New York: Arcade Publishing, 1993), 40.

7. Samuel J. Meisels, "'How Is My Child Doing?'" *Education Week*, 4 August 1993, 54.

8. Ames, Khoju, and Watkins, 29.

9. James Agee and Walker Evans, *Let Us Now Praise Famous Men* (New York: Ballantine Books, 1966), 263.

Patterns to Fit Purpose

1. Dan C. Lortie, *Schoolteacher: A Sociological Study* (Chicago, IL: The University of Chicago Press, 1975), 10.

2. Carnegie Foundation, National Survey of Kindergarten Teachers, 1991; see also Allan Odden, "Class Size and Student Achievement: Research-Based Policy Alternatives," *Educational Evaluation and Policy Analysis* 12, no. 2 (summer 1990), 213–27; and Siobhan Underwood and Linda S. Lumsden, "Class Size," *Research Roundup* 11, no. 1, National Association of Elementary School Principals, Arlington, Virginia, fall 1994.

3. Barbara Nye et al., "The Lasting Benefits Study: A Continuing Analysis of the Effects of Small Class Size in Kindergarten Through Third Grade on Student Achievement Test Scores in Subsequent Grade Levels," Fifth-grade Executive Summary, Center of Excellence for Research in Basic Skills, Tennessee State University, Nashville, TN, 1992, 1.

4. Mary Beth Morgan, personal communication, 2 January 1995; see also Mary Quilling, Linda Parker, David Gray, *Prime Time 1990–91: Six Years Later*, report prepared by PRC, Inc. for the Indiana Department of Education, Indianapolis, IN, 1–7; see also Prime Time materials.

5.   Elam and Gallup, "The 21st Annual Phi Delta Kappa/Gallup Poll of the Public's Attitudes Toward the Public Schools," *Phi Delta Kappan* 71 (September 1989), 45; cited in Barbara Miner, "Students Learn Best in Small Classes," *Rethinking Schools*, January/February 1992, 15.

6.   National Association of Elementary School Principals, Principals' Opinion Survey, The Basic School Concept, 1990.

7.   John I. Goodlad and Robert H. Anderson, *The Nongraded Elementary School*, revised edition (New York: Teachers College Press, Columbia University, 1987), 48–49.

8.   Albert Shanker, "Where We Stand: The Debate on Grouping," American Federation of Teachers advertisement, *The New York Times*, 31 January 1993, sec. E, 7.

     Roberto Gutiérrez and Robert E. Slavin, "Achievement Effects of the Nongraded Elementary School: A Best Evidence Synthesis," *Review of Educational Research* 62, no. 4 (winter 1992), 333–76; see also Roberto Gutiérrez and Robert E. Slavin, *Achievement Effects of the Nongraded School: A Retrospective Review*, report no. 33, Center for Research on Effective Schooling for Disadvantaged Students, The Johns Hopkins University, Baltimore, MD, June 1992.

9.   Edward A. Wynne and Herbert J. Walberg, "Long-term Groupings for Better Learning," *Education Digest*, May 1994, 4, citing *Phi Delta Kappan* 75 (March 1994), 527–30.

10. Kenneth J. Cooper, "Florida Principal Seeks to Instill Sense of Family," *The Washington Post*, 28 October 1991, sec. A, 1, 12.

11. Robert E. Slavin et al., *Success for All: A Relentless Approach to Prevention and Early Intervention in Elementary Schools*, Educational Research Service, Arlington, VA, 1992; see also Bruce Joyce and Emily Calhoun, "Lessons in Learning," *The American School Board Journal* (December 1994), 37–38; and Nancy A. Madden et al., "Success for All," *Phi Delta Kappan* 72 (April 1991), 593–99.

12.   Edward B. Fiske, with Sally Reed and R. Craig Sautter, *Smart Schools, Smart Kids* (New York: Simon and Schuster, 1991), 206.

13.   James P. Comer, "Reinventing Community: A Noted Reformer's Program to Improve Education," speech printed in *Television and Families*, Los Angeles, CA, winter 1990, 49.

14.   Margaret Mead, *Culture and Commitment: A Study of the Generation Gap* (Garden City, NY: Natural History Press, 1970), 2.

15.   Sally Newman and Julie Riess, "Older Workers in Intergenerational Child Care," *Generations Together*, Pittsburgh, PA, July 1990, 18; see also *Generations Together Exchange*, A Newsletter of Intergenerational Issues, Programs, and Research, University Center for Social and Urban Research, University of Pittsburgh, Pittsburgh, PA, Issue 10, winter 1995.

16.   Joy Warner, school visit, January 1995; see also Pat Borden Gubbins, "Young, Old Have Time and Tales to Share," *Mecklenburg Neighbors*, *The Charlotte Observer*, Charlotte, NC, 11 January 1995, sec. M, 1–3.

17.   Darling-Hammond, "Will 21st Century Schools Really Be Different?" 4.

Researchers at a nonprofit group called Public/Private Ventures have found that "an accumulation of longitudinal research suggests that adult relationships—not only with parents and teachers, but with grandparents, neighbors, and other interested adults—are a common factor among children who achieve success despite growing up in disadvantaged and stressful circumstances." Public/Private Ventures has found that intergenerational programs improve the quality of life in schools, as well as improving basic skills. Other researchers have found that making elders partners with children creates an emotional state conducive to learning. But also, the elders are concerned with accountability—they notice when assignments and promises are unfulfilled and they applaud success. Marc Freedman and

Natalie Jaffe, "Elder Mentors: Giving Schools a Hand," NASSP *Bulletin* 76, no. 549, January 1993, 23–24.

Resources to Enrich

1. Carnegie Foundation, *The Condition of Teaching: A State-by-State Analysis, 1990* (Princeton, NJ: Carnegie Foundation, 1990), 213.

2. It has been hard for researchers to document that school library resources make a direct, positive impact on students' academic achievement. A recent, in-depth study of Colorado's public schools, however, did find a direct correlation between student achievement and the size of the library or media center staff, as well as the size of the library's collection. In other words, the better the library, the better the test scores; Keith Curry Lance, Lynda Welborn, and Christine Hamilton-Pennell, *The Impact of School Library Media Centers on Academic Achievement*, Colorado Department of Education, State Library and Adult Education Office, report prepared for the U.S. Department of Education, Office of Educational Research and Improvement Library Programs, September 1992. See also Andrew Trotter, "It's Overdue," *The Executive Educator*, December 1994, 19, 22.

3. Jay Sivin-Kachala and Ellen R. Bialo, *Report on the Effectiveness of Technology in Schools, 1990–1994*; report prepared by Interactive Educational Systems Design, New York, NY, for Software Publishers Association, Washington, DC, 1995.

4. University of California, Irvine, Department of Education, "Analysis of Findings: The Effectiveness of Optical Data Corporation's Science Videodisc Series," Irvine, CA, 7 May 1993.

5. P. Kenneth Komoski, "The 81 Percent Solution: Restructuring Our Schools and Communities for Lifelong Learning," *Education Week*, 26 January 1994, 39.

6.   Seymour Papert, *The Children's Machine: Rethinking School in the Age of the Computer* (New York: Basic Books, 1993), ix.

7.   Jeanne Hayes, personal communication, February 1995; see also Quality Education Data, Inc., *Technology in Public Schools 1993–94*, Denver, CO, 1994.

8.   Bianca Bradbury, "Is Television Mama's Friend or Foe?" *Good Housekeeping*, November 1950, 58, 263.

9.   Schools are restricted in their use of some television programs by program guidelines and copyright set forth by the networks, according to Cable in the Classroom, a nonprofit cable-television industry organization in Alexandria, Virginia. But as of fall 1994, sixty-three percent of all elementary schools across the country are now connected to cable by their local cable company and provided with 525 hours of monthly commercial-free programming at no cost by twenty-seven cable networks such as CNN, Discovery, C-Span, BET, Nickelodeon, A&E, and Bravo. "Teachers can use this programming any way they think best suits their students' needs," said Carol Vernon, at Cable in the Classroom, personal communication, March 1995.

10.   "Cable-Ready Classrooms," *Education Week*, 7 April 1993, 3; citing a Cable in the Classroom report, including a survey by the Cable Alliance for Education, Alexandria, Virginia, 1993.

11.   Jeanne Hayes, personal communication, February 1995; see also Quality Education Data, Inc., *Technology in Public Schools 1993–94*, Denver, CO, 1994.

12.   Tom Lichty, *The Official America Online for Windows Tour Guide*, 2d ed. (Chapel Hill, NC: Ventana Press, 1994).

13.   Only 15 percent of the teachers recently surveyed by the NEA said their access to technology was high. Thirty-eight percent said they were able to get a computer on a part-time basis. Only 8 percent used a fax or modem to exchange information with a colleague. While only 12 percent have a telephone, about 60 percent of the teachers said they need to use a phone several

times a week to talk to parents and school officials; National Education Association, *Technology in the Classroom: A Teacher Perspective*, citing "National Educational Association Communications Survey: Report of the Findings," conducted by Princeton Survey Research Associates for the NEA, Washington, DC, 1993.

14.   Only 30 percent of public elementary schools have Internet access and only 3 percent of all instructional rooms (classrooms, labs, media centers) in public schools are connected to the Internet; Sheila Heaviside et al., *Advanced Telecommunications in U.S. Public Schools, K–12*, U.S. Department of Education, National Center for Education Statistics, February 1995, 3, 12.

15.   Only 27 percent of teachers are currently making final decisions about the purchase of hardware and software for their school; Quality Education Data, Inc., *Educational Technology Trends, 1993–94: QED's 7th Annual Sample Survey of Technology Use and Purchase Plans in U.S. Public Schools*, Denver, CO, 1994, 28.

16.   David McCullough, "A Sense of Proportion," *American Educator* (spring 1995), a publication of American Federation of Teachers, 42.

17.   According to the Association of Youth Museums in Washington, DC, there are about three hundred children's museums across the country, and the number is growing annually; Mary Clancy Haach, personal communication, 31 July 1995. See also Joanne Cleaver, *Doing Children's Museums: A Guide to 265 Hands-On Museums*, revised and expanded edition (Charlotte, VT: Williamson Publishing Co., 1992).

Services for Children

1.   Robert H. Bremner, ed., *Children and Youth in America: A Documentary History*, vol. 2, *1866–1932,* pts. 7 and 8 (Cambridge, MA: Harvard University Press, 1971), 906–10, 916, 1061–62.

Also, Daniel Shea, M.D., "Crisis in the Classroom: How Kids With Poor Health Care Lose in School," *PTA Today*, December 1992 – January 1993, 6–8; and David Hoff, "Students' Poor Health Interferes with Learning, Teachers Say," *Education Daily*, 16 September 1992, 1, 3. Both articles cite a survey of elementary teachers by the American Academy of Pediatrics and the National Parent Teacher Association in which it was found that one in eight young children has a health problem that impairs learning, and most teachers believe the situation is getting worse.

2. In some sections of the country, there are critical nursing shortages. In New York City, eighty-eight nurses were serving one thousand school campuses, for example, down from two hundred nurses in one year as a result of budget cuts; Ellen Flax, "Budgets' Ill Health Prompts Cuts in School Nurses," *Education Week*, 30 October 1991, 10.

3. Carnegie Foundation, *The Condition of Teaching: A State-by-State Analysis, 1990,* Princeton, NJ, 23.

4. Beverly Farquhar, National Association of School Nurses, Inc., personal communication, 25 July 1995. Other studies confirm that psychological, emotional, and learning disorders are rising among children, as are reported cases of abuse and neglect; U.S. House of Representatives, *Health Care: School-Based Health Centers Can Expand Access for Children: A Report to the Chairman, Committee on Government Operations, House of Representatives*, December 1994 (Washington, DC: U.S. General Accounting Office, 1994), 9; also citing *Healthy People 2000: National Health Promotion and Disease Prevention Objectives*, HHS, Public Health Service, 91-50212, September 1990.

5. Louis Harris, "The Public Takes Reform to Heart," *Agenda*, winter 1992, 17.

6. The National Association of School Nurses, Inc., proposes 1 nurse to 750 regular education students and 1 to 250 special education students; see National Health and Education Consortium, *Starting Young: School-Based Health Centers at the Elementary Level*, Washington, DC, 1995.

7. See Calvin R. Stone, "School-Community Collaboration: Comparing Three Initiatives," *Brief to Policymakers*, no. 6, Center on Organization and Restructuring of Schools, University of Wisconsin, School of Education, Madison, WI, fall 1993, 2.

8. Patricia Kramer, quoting Mary Futrell, "Fostering Self-esteem Can Keep Kids Safe and Sound," *PTA Today*, April 1992, 10.

9. Jan Kuhl, "Report on Children's Needs Survey," administered by the Des Moines Elementary Counselors, Des Moines, Iowa, January 1983.

10. "Study: Today's Kids More Troubled," *The Chicago Sun-Times*, 7 December 1993, 30; see also Thomas M. Achenbach and Catherine T. Howell, "Are American Children's Problems Getting Worse? A 13-Year Comparison," *Journal of the American Academy of Child Adolescent Psychiatry* 32, no. 6 (November 1993), 1145–54.

11. David Hilfiker, M.D., *Not All of Us Are Saints: A Doctor's Journey with the Poor* (New York: Hill & Wang, 1994), 136.

12. Constance Kaprowicz, "50-State Survey, State Policy for Elementary School Counselors," National Conference of State Legislatures, Denver, CO, 1992. Also, the ratio in *elementary* schools is currently one counselor for five hundred to eight hundred students, according to Pamela Gabbard, elementary vice president, American School Counselor Association, personal communication, Alexandria, VA, 24 July 1995.

13. Felicia R. Lee, "In New York Schools, Guidance Counselors Are Facing Tough Challenges," *The New York Times*, 12 February 1990, sec. A, 17.

14. See "The Sea of Life Is So Large While a Child's Boat Is So Small," Smoother Sailing, elementary guidance and counseling program, Des Moines Public Schools, Des Moines, IA.

15. A recent report called *Prisoners of Time* concluded that, "Time is learning's warden. Our time-bound mentality has fooled us all into believing that schools can educate all of the people all of

the time in a school year of 180 six-hour days. The consequence of our self-deception has been to ask the impossible of our students. We expect them to learn as much as their counterparts abroad in only half the time." National Education Commission on Time and Learning, *Prisoners of Time* (Washington, DC: GPO, April 1994), 7.

16. Nearly two million grade school children with employed mothers now come home every afternoon to an empty house, according to recent Census Bureau figures; Martin O'Connell, personal communication, 27 July 1995. See also, Lynne M. Casper, Mary Hawkins, and Martin O'Connell, *Who's Minding the Kids? Child Care Arrangements: Fall 1991*, U.S. Bureau of the Census, Current Population Reports (Washington, DC: GPO, 1994).

17. See Deborah L. Cohen, "Hawaii Program for After-School Care Irks Private Firms," *Education Week*, 14 March 1990, 1.

18. Charles Ballinger, personal communication, 23 July 1995, and materials from National Association for Year-Round Education, San Diego, CA.

19. See Patricia Gandara and Judy Fish, "Year-Round Schooling as an Avenue to Major Structural Reform," *Educational Evaluation and Policy Analysis* 16 (spring 1994), 67–85.

20. "Helping Students Who Fall Behind," report no. 22, Center for Research on Effective Schooling for Disadvantaged Students, The Johns Hopkins University, Baltimore, MD, 1992.

21. Sophronia Scott Gregory, reported by Ann Blackman and Bonnie I. Rochman, "Everyone into the School!" *Time*, 1 August 1994, 48–49.

22. Connie Leslie, with Karen Springen, "Schools That Never Close," *Newsweek*, 15 May 1989, 60.

23. See Robert L. Crowson and William Lowe Boyd, "Coordinated Services for Children: Designing Arks for Storms and Seas Unknown," *American Journal of Education* 101 (February 1993), 140–79.

24. Allan Shedlin, Jr., personal communication, November 1994; see also Susan Hlesciak Hall, "At the Heart of the Matter: Would a 'Hub' of Needed Services Improve Learning in Your Community's Schools?" *Network for Public Schools* 17, no. 1, National Committee for Citizens in Education, 1991.

25. See Charlotte-Mecklenburg Board of Education, "Report of the Community Task Force," May 14, 1991; also, minutes of the meeting of the Children's Services Network, Charlotte, NC, 17 October 1991.

26. Boyer, *Ready to Learn*, 130–31.

The Core Virtues

1. Joy Elmer Morgan, *Horace Mann: His Ideas and Ideals* (Washington, DC: National Home Library Foundation, 1936). See also Kristen J. Amundson, *Teaching Values and Ethics: Problems and Solutions,* an AASA Critical Issues Report, American Association of School Administrators, Arlington, VA, 1991, 18.

2. Robert Michaelsen, *Piety in the Public School* (New York: The Macmillan Company, 1970), 77, citing Mary Tyler Peabody Mann, *Life and Works of Horace Mann* V (Boston: Lee and Shepard; New York: C.T. Dillingham, 1891), 73; cf. IV, 283.

3. William Raspberry, "At a Loss for an Answer," *The Washington Post*, 10 January 1994, sec. A, 15.

4. See Jean Piaget, *The Moral Judgment of the Child,* trans. Marjorie Gabain (New York: The Free Press, 1965).

5. George Steiner, *Language and Silence: Essays on Language, Literature, and the Inhuman* (New York: Atheneum, 1967), ix–x.

6. Robert Coles, *The Spiritual Life of Children* (Boston: Houghton Mifflin Company, 1990), xvii.

7. In 1952, when the U.S. Supreme Court ruled such "released time" constitutional—provided the public school is in no way

involved—Justice William O. Douglas wrote: "We are a religious people whose institutions presuppose a Supreme Being. We guarantee the freedom to worship as one chooses. . . . When the state encourages the religious instruction or cooperates with religious authorities by adjusting the schedule of public events to sectarian needs, it follows the best of our traditions. For it then respects the religious nature of our people and accommodates the public service to their spiritual needs." See John W. Whitehead, *The Rights of Religious Persons in Public Education* (Wheaton, IL: Crossway Books, 1994), 201, citing *Zorach v. Clauson* (343 US 306, 313–14, 1952).

8. Ellie Ashford, "Interest Grows for Weekday Religious Education Programs," *School Board News* 14, no. 24, National School Boards Association, 27 December 1994, 1–5.

9. Johnson and Immerwahr, *First Things First: What Americans Expect from the Public Schools*, 12.

   The 1994 Gallup survey reflected the increasing interest in character education in the schools. An increasing percentage of Americans believe that schools should be teaching values and ethical behavior. Fifty-seven percent of public school parents believe character education should be taught in the public schools, up from 45 percent in 1987; Elam, Rose, and Gallup, "The 26th Annual Phi Delta Kappa/Gallup Poll," *Phi Delta Kappan* 76 (September 1994), 49.

10. Wilson and Corcoran, "212 Successful Schools," *Streamlined Seminar* 7, no. 1, September 1988, 1–2; and Research for Better Schools, *Places Where Children Succeed*, Philadelphia, PA, 1987.

11. William Kilpatrick, *Why Johnny Can't Tell Right from Wrong: Moral Illiteracy and the Case for Character Education* (New York: Simon & Schuster, 1992), 225–26.

12. A recent poll, in fact, found that almost 70 percent of the American public thinks it would be possible to get people in their community to agree on a set of basic values that would be taught in the public schools; Elam, Rose, and Gallup, "The 25th

Annual Phi Delta Kappa/Gallup Poll of the Public's Attitudes Toward the Public Schools," *Phi Delta Kappan* 75 (October 1993), 145.

13. E. D. Hirsch, Jr., *Cultural Literacy: What Every American Needs to Know* (Boston: Houghton Mifflin Company, 1987), 103, 136.

14. David Hoff, "AASA: Schools Need Not Shy Away From Teaching Values," *Education Daily*, 14 February 1995, 2.

15. Ibid.

16. John O'Neil, "ASCD Joins Partnership," ASCD *Update* 35, no. 4, Association for Supervision and Curriculum Development, May 1993, 1, 6.

17. See James Q. Wilson, *The Moral Sense* (New York: The Free Press, 1993); William J. Bennett, ed., *The Book of Virtues: A Treasury of Great Moral Stories* (New York: Simon & Schuster, 1993), 13.

18. Jim Kennelly, "Education: Reading, Writing, and Doing Right," *USA Weekend*, 19–21 August 1994, 10; and Charles L. Scott, "Shaping Character," *The American School Board Journal* (December 1992), 28–30.

19. Dayton Public Schools, personal communication, 24 February 1995; see also "Greater Dayton Community to Support and Participate in Dayton Schools' Character Education Program," press release, Dayton Public Schools, 9 September 1994.

20. The Network for Educational Development, "Personal Responsibility Education Process" handbook, Cooperating School Districts, St. Louis, Missouri, 18.

21. The Network for Educational Development, Personal Responsibility Education Program, PREP *Update* 5, no. 2, spring 1994, 2; see also Bob Moody and Linda McKay, "PREP: A Process, Not a Recipe," *Educational Leadership*, November 1993, 28–30.

22. Kae E. Keister, personal communication, 2 August 1994; and Milford Board of Education "Values Committee" materials, Milford, DE.

Living with Purpose

1. Kristen J. Amundson, *Teaching Values and Ethics: Problems and Solutions*, AASA Critical Issues Report, American Association of School Administrators, Arlington, VA, 1991, 36–38.

2. William Kilpatrick, "The Moral Power of Good Stories," *American Educator* (summer 1993), 24–35.

3. Kenneth L. Woodward, "What is Virtue?" *Newsweek*, 13 June 1994, 39; see also *The Ethics of Aristotle: The Nicomachean Ethics*, translated by J.A.K. Thomson (Baltimore, MD: Penguin Books, 1953).

4. William Damon, *Greater Expectations: Overcoming the Culture of Indulgence in America's Homes and Schools* (New York: The Free Press, 1995), 38.

5. More than two hundred school districts around the nation already make service to the community part of the educational program; Jessica Portner, "On Assignment: At Your Service," *Education Week*, 23 November 1994, 19–20.

6. Linda Jenkins, personal communication, September 1994; see also *Elucidation: Profiles to Understand the Role of Student Service in School Improvement*, The StarServe Foundation, 1993, 3–16.

7. Robert K. Greenleaf, *Servant Leadership: A Journey into the Nature of Legitimate Power and Greatness* (New York: Paulist Press, 1976), 250.

Index